Kirstin von G

111 Shops
in London
that You
Shouldn't Miss

(111)

emons:

I thank all the shopkeepers for the wonderful interviews and
Niko, Juli, Mandel, Gundi and Yoda for their support.

Bibliographical Information of the Deutsche Nationalbibliothek
The Deutsche Nationalbibliothek lists this publication
in the Deutsche Nationalbibliografie; detailed bibliographical
data are available on the internet at http://dnb.d-nb.de

© Emons Verlag GmbH
All rights reserved
© all photos: Kirstin von Glasow, except: Biscuiteers by Biscuiteers
Design: TIZIAN BOOKS, based on a design
by Lübekke / Naumann / Thoben
Editing: Margaret Hiley
Typesetting and digital processing: Gerd Wiechcinski
Maps / Cartography: altancicek.design, www.altancicek.de
Maps based on data by Openstreetmap, © Openstreet Map-participants, ODbL
Printing and Binding: B.O.S.S Medien GmbH, Goch
Printed in Germany 2014
ISBN 978-3-95451-341-3
Second edition

For best informations
about emons publications,
please subscribe to our free newsletter
at www.emons-verlag.de

Foreword

When our children were young we often went to Portobello Market. One Saturday I was looking at something at a stall in Golborne Road and when I turned around, my son, who was around three years old at the time, had vanished. I panicked and ran around like a headless chicken calling his name. Immediately several of the shopkeepers came running from their shops and started to help me look for him. My son was soon found and the impression of their helpfulness and interest has stayed with me ever since.

I experienced the same genuine interest when I carried out the research for this book years later. The shopkeepers of the small independent shops I visited were not only helpful and friendly because they wanted to sell something to their customers; they knew their names and they wanted to sell them high quality goods because they were proud of their products. Selling things was not merely a monetary transaction to them, but part of their life and what they believed in.

Like all big cities, London has a large turnover: many shops close and open every year, but in hardly any other metropolis will you find an equally high percentage of traditional family businesses that have existed for hundred years and more – from boot and hat makers, mash & pie shops to producers of buttonholes and bell foundries. Although London is one of the most important financial capitals in the world, Londoners are traditional at heart. They love to go to the same shops again and again. They also love all things old!

Vintage shops, from fashion and antique furniture to architectural antiques, play an important role in English culture and this is why they are well represented in this book. Innovative businesses, which sell new products or find new ways of distributing their goods, add their spice to the dish that is the independent shop scene. London's ability to constantly reinvent itself while retaining a respect for tradition and continuity makes it such an exciting city both to visit and to live in.

111 Shops

1 @work
Ring with a twist

The industrial glass and steel display cases in this shop are nearly invisible so as not to distract from the quirky contemporary jewellery displayed here.

@work is jointly owned and run by Adele Tipler and Joanna Butler. Both of them are jewellers; Joanna studied at Glasgow School of Art, Adele at the Royal College of Art in London. Adele became known as a metal milliner for her large sculptural headpieces. Today she makes jewellery using brightly coloured irregular semi-precious stones. Joanna mixes silver and gold. Her pieces are often hammered and incorporate semi-precious stones.

Adele and Joanna used to share a workshop in Hoxton, selling their work to different outlets, but felt isolated and out of touch with their customers. They established the Gallery in 1998, not only to show their own work but also to showcase contemporary jewellery designers they liked. The customers that visit the shop in Brick Lane are so diverse that Adele and Joanna can sell a range of very different jewellery, including quirky pieces or items using unusual materials like wood, silicon, antler bone, paper resin or nylon. There are the textile pieces of Miwa Vicary, ranging from an animal-head necklace to soft tea cups as hairbands, or the cufflinks and necklaces by Bug that look like old-fashioned record players, keyboards or headphones. Comocuando produces weird creature necklaces, thrown together from parts of different animals with human legs and feet.

@work has become so successful that Adele and Joanna were able to open another shop in Pimlico in 2006, with a basement workshop where they do jewellery courses and bespoke orders. On some of the courses you can make a ring in a day, others are for betrothed couples who make each other wedding rings. You can also bring in your old gold jewellery and they will melt it down and create something new. A ring with a twist, perhaps?

Address 160 Brick Lane, E1 6RU, Tel. +44(0)2073770597, www.atworkgallery.co.uk, sales@atworkgallery.co.uk | Public Transport Circle, District, Hammersmith Line, Stop Aldgate East | Opening Hours Mon–Sat 11am–6pm, Sun 2.30pm–5.30pm | Tip At Spitalfields Arts Market (Brushfield Street, from Thurs-Sun, once or twice a month) you can buy affordable art directly from up-and-coming artists.

2 Andy & Tuly

For every man and every shirt

If you can't find suitable cufflinks in Andy and Tuly's little shop in elegant Princes Arcade, then you won't anywhere, because they stock over 10,000 of them. Tuly originally comes from Vietnam. A tailor by trade, she worked for many years in Jermyn Street and for Liberty, the renowned department store. Besides cufflinks she also sells jewellery, waistcoats and ties she designs and embroiders herself.

In 2000 she opened the shop, which is now the oldest shop in the arcade, with her husband Andy, who manages their second store in Charing Cross Road. In the beginning they only had a small selection of classic cufflinks. Soon customers began to ask for different models; they started to offer a wider selection and today there is virtually no man or shirt they don't have a matching pair of cufflinks for.

Flags are very popular: from Brazil to India, they stock many different countries from all over the world. You can either choose a matching pair or have any combination of two different flags; a useful present for gentlemen who travel a lot – but choose carefully, because the wrong combination of flags could have catastrophic consequences! You can't make any mistakes if you buy a couple of animal cufflinks: from pugs to mice and dolphins to bees, you'll find the right animal for the gentleman in question. Or would you prefer a London souvenir? Andy and Tuly stock taxis, buses, underground signs and phone boxes. Many men also enjoy tools like drills and hammers, or perhaps trains and tractors? If you can't decide, buy one with a saying on it – or even better: working watches as cufflinks! And if you bring your own coins, you can have a pair of cufflinks custom-made from them.

The prices are as varied as the models. They are not always expensive, but if you want diamonds you will of course have to spend a bit more. Whatever your taste or purse may be – Andy and Tuly will find something that suits you!

Address 12 Princes Arcade, Jermyn Street, SW1Y 6DS, Tel. +44(0)2074943259, www.andytuly.co.uk/Cufflinks, nguyen@andytuly.fsnet.co.uk | **Public Transport** Bakerloo, Piccadilly Line, Stop Piccadilly Circus | **Opening Hours** Mon – Sat 9.30am – 6.30pm, Sun 11.30am – 4.30pm | **Tip** Go to the Royal Academy (Burlington House, Piccadilly) to see their latest exhibitions.

3 Angels
Transformations

Behind a narrow shop window in the heart of London's theatre district there hides one of the biggest costume and fancy dress hire businesses in the world. Now in the sixth generation, the family business hires out costumes for stage and film as well as helping anyone wanting to go to a fancy dress party to realise their Cinderella dreams.

Andy has worked for Angels for 15 years and manages the business in Shaftesbury Avenue. He explains that the professional costume hire for film, TV and stage has been located in a warehouse in Hendon since 2002, whereas the one in Soho is smaller, more concentrated and caters for the needs of private and corporate customers. The quality of the costumes is the same in both places. 34 of the films Angels provides costumes for have won Oscars in this category, including films like »Titanic«, »Shakespeare in Love«, »Gladiator« and »Anna Karenina«.

Here in Soho, between cinemas and theatres, Angels sells ready-made costumes and offers a made-to-measure costume service. The large selection of ready-made costumes available ranges from beer bottles and hot dogs to naughty costumes for hen or stag parties. When the hire costumes are returned, they are professionally cleaned and repaired if necessary. So why not go inside and come out as Harry Potter, Eliza Doolittle or the Great Gatsby? The professional team will make sure the costume fits perfectly and that you have the right accessories like swords, glasses or wands. The experts here know the latest trends, often influenced by successful films. Thanks to Johnny Depp, the most popular costume is a pirate disguise. The costumers also love challenges, even if a mixture of Elvis, Darth Vader and Regency gentleman is wanted.

»The most important thing,« says Andy, »is that customers feel comfortable in their costumes and look fantastic.« What would you like to be: a Victorian punk or a medieval dandy? Angels will help you to transform yourself!

Address 119 Shaftesbury Avenue, WC2H 8AE, Tel. +44(0)2078365678,
www.fancydress.com, info@fancydress.com | Public Transport Northern, Piccadilly,
Central Line, Stop Tottenham Court Road, Leicester Square | Opening Hours Mon, Tues
9.30am–5.30pm, Weds 10.30am–7pm, Thurs, Fri 9.30am–5.30pm | Tip Buy a ticket for
the theatre and watch Angels' costumes in action!

4 Aperture

A beautiful camera shop

Shops selling photo cameras and camera equipment are often scary places. The lighting is too bright, the carpets are too ugly and staff easily lose patience if you don't know exactly what you're looking for. Luckily, none of this applies to Aperture on Rathbone Place. Here you will find wooden floors, old mahogany shop counters and beautiful old Leicas, Nikons or Rolleiflex cameras in display cabinets.

The shop sells, buys and repairs mechanical cameras. Customers can also develop and print their analog films here. They can sit down at tables in the back of the shop and examine their potential purchases thoroughly. Everyone who works in the shop has lots of time to chat with the customers about cameras or indeed anything under the sun.

Aperture began as a hobby because shop owner Patrick Tang enjoyed photography. He started to buy cameras abroad and sell them to dealers in the UK. Patrick describes himself as »not a very good photographer«, but he loves to sell things he really likes and his idea to create a beautiful camera shop has proven to be very successful. Rathbone Place is already his second shop. He opened the first over ten years ago on Museum Street in Bloomsbury. Mechanical cameras fascinate Patrick not only because of the technical differences between film and digital photography. For him, a photographer who uses a mechanical camera is far more involved in the creative process of taking a picture. The number of pictures you can take at a time is limited and the photographer will compose each picture more carefully.

Most clients are camera enthusiasts, but some are professionals who enjoy photographing with mechanical cameras in their spare time. The mostly male customers often spend a long time in the shop looking a camera over. It's not uncommon for people to come back to the shop again and again and even buy the same camera they sold here some months or years ago – just because Aperture is so beautiful!

Address 27 Rathbone Place, W1T 1JE, Tel. +44(0)2074361015, www.apertureuk.com, 27@apertureuk.com | Public Transport Northern, Central Line, Stop Goodge Street, Tottenham Court Road | Opening Hours Mon–Fri 11am–7pm, Sat 12pm–7pm | Tip At Hobgoblin Music (24 Rathbone Place) you will find a great selection of folk music instruments.

5 Aquatic Design Centre
The Indian Ocean in your living room

To visit the Aquatic Design Centre is as good as visiting an aquarium – with the additional bonus of knowledgeable advice about fish-keeping! So even if you don't have an aquarium, it's well worth coming here to be inspired by the amazing variety of aquatic life!

The Aquatic Design Centre has the biggest number of tanks installed in a shop in London. On two floors you wander past tanks and aquariums filled with freshwater fish, marine fish, corals, reptiles and amphibians, aquatic plants and freshwater shrimp. You can also buy all the equipment you need to create and maintain your own aquarium. Greg Czyrak, who has managed the shop for six years, knows everything about the latest trends in fish-keeping. Like nearly all the employees in the shop, he kept fish as a child and his passion for aquatic life only grew stronger over the years. He likes planter tanks that contain only plants and is very much into freshwater shrimp, the latest craze in fish-keeping. Greg explains that fish–keeping has changed a lot over the last 20 years. With increasing scientific knowledge about fish and their habitats, different natural environments can be recreated on a small scale. Using pumps and adjusting temperature and lighting – for example emulating different lunar phases – the Aquatic Design Centre is able to recreate a huge range of environments, from the Amazon to an Indonesian stream and the Indian Ocean.

They design and maintain aquariums that look like living works of art for big companies and institutions, ranging from Harrods to Holloway Prison. They have turned a car into a fish tank, installed a 15,000 litre coral reef aquarium, and designed shark tanks for celebrities. But even if you are a first-time fish-keeper, they will still provide you with all the knowledge and equipment you need. Many customers come to the shop regularly to have a cup of coffee and look at the fish. But beware – fish-keeping can be addictive and before you know it, you might have the Indian Ocean in your living room!

Address 107–109 Great Portland Street, W1W 6QG, Tel. +44 (0)2075806764 |
Public Transport Circle, Hammersmith, Metropolitan Line, Stop Great Portland Street |
Opening Hours Mon–Thurs 10am–8pm, Fri 10am–7pm, Sat 10am–6pm, Sun 11am–5pm |
Tip Take your afternoon tea in the Palm Court of the Langham Hotel, where Lady Gaga
stays when she is in London.

6 Architectural Forum
Heat your house in style

Ever dreamt of sitting in front of a Georgian or Victorian fireplace, watching the flames while sipping a glass of wine? Architectural Forum can make this dream come true, as it specialises in reclaiming and restoring antique fireplaces. Whether you are dreaming of an Adam's Style ornately carved wooden surround or an early 19th-century simple mantelpiece made from Yorkstone, the shop has it all and more besides. It also stocks reclaimed cast iron radiators in all heights, sizes and styles in a large range of finishes. If you know the measurements of the room and the space where the radiator will go, Architectural Forum will make them according to any style you require. Once you've installed your heating, if you find you have a bit of money left, you can purchase an old-fashioned Butler sink or a stone gargoyle for your garden. You'll find a great choice of reclaimed items in their yard or in the showroom.

Jason Davies founded the architectural salvage company in 1988. He already knew a lot about the profession because his father was an antiques dealer, but he took the business to a whole new dimension, doing retail as well as trade. Salvaging parts of old houses can be tricky because there's often little time before the building is demolished. Working with its sister company V&V Reclamation, Architectural Forum has been involved in some spectacular salvages including removing pieces from the Baltic Exchange, which has now been replaced by the Gherkin.

Jason likes the diversity of his work, which ranges from demolishing a Tibetan gambling shop to providing the Portland stone for a Swedish baroque-style mansion: »You never know what you get when you come to a demolishing site!« Asked what style is selling best at the moment, he says: »At the moment industrial/warehouse style is still in fashion, but this will change.« His own taste veers more towards Georgian mahogany. But whatever you prefer, he will help you to heat and furnish your house in style!

Address 312 Essex Road, N1 3AX, Tel. +44(0)2077040982, www.thearchitecturalforum.com, info@thearchitecturalforum.com | **Public Transport** Victoria Line, Stop Highbury, Islington | **Opening Hours** Mon–Thurs 9am–5pm, Fri–Sat 9am–6pm, Sun 11am–4pm | **Tip** Parallel to Essex Road you can find New River Walk, a small man-made park running along the remnants of an old aqueduct – a hidden oasis of calm.

7__Arthur Beale

Do you own a boat?

No? Don't worry, it's not strictly necessary to possess a boat in order to find something you like at Arthur Beale's. Whether you love brass lamps, need a rope to build a swing or a tree house, or just admire the beauty and functionality of maritime objects, go and visit the shop. Arthur Beale is a yacht chandler, stocking everything to do with boats: ropes, hooks in all sizes and shapes, barometers, shackles, flags, boat paints and varnishes.

You can also get porthole mirrors, brass whistles, small telescopes and a wide array of other things that float your boat! Customers who are not boat owners can still buy a ship bell and – by hanging it in the kitchen or any other place in the house – convert it into a house bell. You can also have your name or other inscriptions engraved into it. If this still sounds too nautical for you, just buy a set of brass hooks; they are really useful and look good in every room.

Cecil Coleman has worked here for over 55 years and has seen it all. He started at Arthur Beale's because he liked sailing and the sea. »The shop«, he explains, »started long before my time. It has already been here for 110 years but it began as a rope maker 400 years ago. It turned into a yacht chandler when synthetic ropes came up and rope making was industrialised.«

During his long time working for the yacht chandler Mr Coleman has equipped many boats, including the dinghy that won Olympic Gold 30 years ago. Many of his customers are still boat owners, but an increasing number of people buy things here for other purposes than boating. Art students and performance artists come here to get inspiration and once someone bought several items to furnish his dungeon. The costume designer of the musical »The Lion King« bought many metres of rope to make a costume. Regardless of whether you own a boat or not, it is definitely worth coming here. Let your creative flag fly!

Address 194 Shaftesbury Avenue, WC2H 8JP, Tel. +44(0)2078369034 | **Public Trans-port** Central, Northern Line, Stop Tottenham Court Road | **Opening Hours** Mon–Fri 9am–6pm, Sat 9.30am–1pm | **Tip** Science fiction fans find comics, DVDs and action figures of their heroes at Forbidden Planet (179 Shaftesbury Avenue).

8 Bageriet
Take a fika!

If you walk past this little shop near Covent Garden at 11am, you will be stopped in your tracks by the wonderful smell of cinnamon and baking. Why not go inside and have a coffee and cinnamon bun? This is what Swedish people do at this time of day: they take a »fika«, a coffee break. In Sweden, fika is a social institution. Together with your friends, colleagues or family, you take a break from work to drink coffee and eat something sweet, usually a »Vetebröd«, a sweet spiced yeast bread. The Swedes love their pastries and the average Swede eats the equivalent of 316 cinnamon buns a year.

Daniel Karlsson and Sven-Gunnar Appelgren, the two Swedish bakers behind Bageriet, opened the shop in April 2013. Daniel was first inspired to start baking by his grandmother, who made the most extraordinary pastries. He had to take one year of baking during his training as a cook and became hooked. He met Sven-Gunnar when they were both working in a bakery in Stockholm. Both of them are passionate about baking and very proud of the Swedish cake tradition – and rightly so, for the cakes and biscuits they make are simply heavenly. For example, you could try the Swedish national cake, »Princess cake«, a light sponge filled with raspberry jam, custard and cream, all covered with a layer of apple-green marzipan. Bageriet also makes different kinds of biscuits: spiced almond, double chocolate or vanilla biscuits with apricot jam and sugar crystals.

Did you know that a good Swedish housewife has to make seven different types of biscuits to serve with coffee? If you are here in the winter, you can have »Klenäter«, a deep-fried specialty eaten at Christmas, or »Semlor«, wheat buns filled with cream eaten between Christmas and Easter. No sweet tooth? Well, then you can have some »Smörgastartor«, a savoury sandwich cake filled with prawn, ham or cheese salad. Enjoy your fika!

Address 24 Rose Street, WC2E 9EA, Tel. +44(0)2072400000, www.bageriet.co.uk, info@bageriet.co.uk, | **Public Transport** Northern, Piccadilly Line, Stop Leicester Square | **Opening Hours** Mon – Fri 9am – 7pm, Sat 10am – 7pm | **Tip** St Paul's Church in Bedford Street is also called the »actors' church« because of its connection to the surrounding theatres. The garden is a haven of quiet in busy Covent Garden.

9__Barn the Spoon
Trees, spoons, axes and knives

As you would probably rather drive on Hackney Road than walk along it leisurely, it is easy to miss Barn the Spoon. »It's a destination shop,« says Barnaby Carder, also known as Barn the Spoon, who founded the shop in 2012. »Not a lot of people walk past, but when they drive past they check us out on the internet and we have got a lot of publicity lately.« No wonder, because the shop is basically a big shop window, behind which you can see Barn or one of his apprentices sitting on a chair carving wooden spoons, mountains of wood shavings gathering beneath them.

Here you can buy wooden spoons – nothing else. If you think that is not enough, just talk to Barn! »Everyone uses them, they're the first things we feed ourselves with. More complex to work with than bowls – those are beautiful too – but spoons have an additional handle. They are the high end of woodcraft!« From Barn, you can learn this and more besides about spoons. He also teaches spoon making in evening, one-day or one-week courses.

Barn has been a woodworker his whole life. He was apprenticed to a furniture maker and later traveled the country, sleeping in the woods and carving and selling spoons. Barn loves trees and sources most of his wood from nearby parks in London, having permission from the council to remove certain trees. Barn uses different kinds of unseasoned green wood to make spoons and also is very interested in the utensil's history. Most of his designs are based on traditional forms like the medieval drinking spoon, a Shakespearean spoon, a Roma spoon or just a simple cooking spoon. His tools: an axe, a knife and a bent knife, as simple as the spoons he makes. Trees, spoons, axes and knives are the fixtures in Barn's life, and everything else has to be accommodated around them. Usually Barn is more comfortable talking about spoons than talking about himself, but for some people spoon-making even becomes a therapy. Spoons do that to you!

Address 260 Hackney Road, E2 7SJ, Tel. +44(0)7950751811, barnthespoon.blogspot.co.uk |
Public Transport London Overground towards Crystal Palace, Stop Hoxton | Opening
Hours Fri 10am–5pm, Sat 10am–5pm, Sun 10am–5pm | Tip The Geffrye Museum
(136 Kingsland Road) shows the history of the home, with several rooms from different
periods as well as period gardens.

10__Beauty & the bib

I love my strawberry bib

The signature bib made by beauty & the bib is a strawberry. The founder and owner of the business, Lara Boyle, just loves strawberries: their soft silhouette, their colour, their seeds and their little green collar inspired the mother of four to create a strawberry bib. She uses soft cotton terry toweling and each bib has three layers of fabric with interlining between them – so no matter how much a baby dribbles, it won't get wet clothes or a wet chest. The bibs are machine washable, dry easily and look beautiful.

Lara started in 2004 with a stall at Greenwich Market. Encouraged by the positive response, she exhibited at trade shows and when her stock threatened to choke her house she moved it to an industrial unit. The business, which had started from home, expanded and she found distributors in Japan, Italy, Poland, Denmark and Sweden, finally opening her shop in Greenwich Market in 2008. Here she sells not only seventeen different-coloured strawberry bibs but also apple, star, heart or cupcake-shaped bibs. There are models for every occasion. The bibs can be personalised: embroidered with the baby's name or crowns, bananas and bumblebees. Others show »I love …« messages, from »I love my cat« to »I love Greenwich Market« or even royal allusions like »I love my uncle Harry«!

The special needs bibs they stock are larger and can be worn by older children. Lara has also designed a model to support a children's cancer charity. All the bibs are packaged in their own organza bags. The shop also sells baby clothes like onesies – some of them matching the bibs – baby hats or London-themed playsuits. Some of the garments come from carefully selected other brands, complementing the beauty & the bib products. For Lara it is really important to believe in what she sells and she is passionate about her products. If babies could choose their own bib message, it would surely say: »I love my strawberry bib!«

Address Unit 27b, Tarves Way, SE10 9JU, Tel. +44(0)2082930529, www.beautyandthebib.com, lara@beautyandthebib.com | Public Transport DLR towards Lewisham, Stop Cutty Sark | Opening Hours Mon–Fri 11am–5pm, Sat, Sun 10am–6pm | Tip Visit the Painted Hall in the Royal Naval College Greenwich (King William Walk). Designed by Christopher Wren, it was an eating hall for naval veterans.

11 Benjamin Pollock's Toyshop

Play with paper

Narrow stairs in Covent Garden Market lead up to Benjamin Pollock's Toyshop, which sells paper toy theatres and other traditional toys. These miniature stages go back to the Regency era, when it was fashionable to have your own miniature version of the newest play. Toy theatres have always been important to British culture – so much so that Robert Louis Stevenson wrote an essay about Pollock's Toy Shop.

The shop, which has been located here since the 1980s, goes back to Benjamin Pollock who married the daughter of a publisher and printer over 100 years ago and started to print and sell toy theatres shortly after. Years after his death Marguerite Fawdry bought all of his shop's original stock. She opened Pollock's Toy Museum and later the shop in Covent Garden. Today the shop is independent of the museum but continues the tradition of telling stories with paper. 100 years ago a toy theatre fulfilled the same function as a DVD today. After seeing a play in the theatre, you could buy it as a paper model, which you could either paint yourself or buy hand-painted or printed. Later it often came in form of a book, out of which the different parts were cut out and put together. Voilà – a private little theatre all of your own! Over time this function was lost and theatres became children's toys, but their fascination is still there.

Simon Seddon, Pollock's manager, got hooked when he was a teenager. Someone gave him such a book and he spent days putting it together. »Toy theatres have a strange appeal,« Simon says, »not only because they are models of a big theatre but they create their own microcosm that comes to live with a person looking at them.« A Spanish theatre, a Victorian model or a tiny stage in a matchbox: a lot of the models can be put together in half an hour. Others need a bit more patience. Go ahead, you're the director: create your own play with paper!

Address 44 The Market, Covent Garden, WC2E 8RF, Tel. +44(0)2073797866,
www.pollocks-coventgarden.co.uk, info@pollocks-coventgarden.co.uk | Public Transport
Piccadilly Line, Stop Covent Garden | Opening Hours Mon–Sat 10.30am–6pm, Sun
11am–4pm | Tip Fans of the opera, visit the Royal Opera House (Covent Garden)!

12 Biscuiteers

Write a biscuit!

The jolly outside of the Biscuiteers boutique in Notting Hill with its striped awning invites you to come closer and be tempted inside by the gorgeous iced biscuits, gingerbread men and women in the shop window.

Biscuiteers started as an online company in 2007 when founders Harriet Hastings and Stevie Congdon had the idea of sending biscuits instead of cards: »Why send flowers when you can send biscuits instead?« They spent a long time experimenting as they wanted the biscuits to taste and look equally beautiful. The ingredients are sourced from two British suppliers and they have three main recipes: chocolate and vanilla all year round and an allspice biscuit at Christmas.

Here, biscuits are created as collections for every occasion and every season: from Easter egg to Christmas biscuits; tins containing safari animals or cats; gingerbread supermen, batmen or princesses, who congratulate you on your new house, your new baby or say sorry; they even have a first-aid biscuit tin containing a band aid biscuit and a medicine bottle biscuit among others – guaranteed recovery included! A collection of mini London sights, from Tower Bridge to the London Eye, makes a lovely souvenir. Biscuiteers proved that they can think big as well when they were commissioned to design the Selfridges main Christmas window with an edible »Lost London« cityscape, made from 353 kilograms of gingerbread!

Besides biscuits, they sell delicious and beautifully hand-iced chocolates in flavours like crème caramel or cinnamon toffee apple and honey. You can also buy amazing cakes, which you can personalise like the biscuits and chocolates. Would you like to have a go at icing yourself? Attend a masterclass at the school of icing or pop into the icing café! Before leaving, you really should write a biscuit to your loved one!

Address 194 Kensington Park Road, W11 2ES, Tel. +44(0)2077278096, www.biscuiteers.com | **Public Transport** Circle, District, Hammersmith Line, Stop Ladbroke Grove | **Opening Hours** Mon 10am–5pm, Tues–Sat 10am–6pm, Sun 11am–5pm | **Tip** At the corner of Kensington Park Road and Elgin Crescent you'll find Harper & Tom's, a lovely flower kiosk that always has fresh, seasonal blooms.

13 Blade Rubber Stamps
Stamp Art!

Only a stone's throw from the British Museum, Blade Rubber Stamps sells rubber stamps, inkpads and other necessary equipment for stamping and stamp-making as well as scrapbooking materials and stencils.

The shop has something for everyone. If you are looking for a London souvenir that's also a bit unusual, you'll find it here: from the London Eye to a postbox, taxi, bus or a sign saying »Keep calm and carry on«, Blade Rubber stocks a variety of rubber stamps with typical London motifs. If you are a card-maker or an artist who never learned to draw, the shop has wonderful artistic stamps from companies like Paper Artsy or Crafty Individuals. If you loved playing at post office as a child and or want to go »postal«, you can get those indispensable post stamps here. Scrapbook makers will find scrapbooking paper, punches, peel-offs, inks, embellishments and many other things to create amazing albums. So who is behind this haven for creatively-minded people?

It all started when Graham Adams was selling stamps at Camden Market. He met Kaye Flack while out walking his dogs and everything else developed from there. They opened the shop in 1993. Today Graham and Kaye mainly deal with the workshop, where they design and produce Blade Rubber's own range of stamps. Deirdre Thomas, who has worked for them for 20 years, manages the shop. Besides selling stamps, their »made to order stamp service« offers you the opportunity to try your hand at designing stamps without starting from scratch. Do you need an art stamp for your CDs, or would you like to design a stamp for your business or wedding? You can email your own art work to Blade Rubber Stamps or use their »online stamp designer« and your stamp will be ready in only a few days! On Saturdays the shop offers a variety of craft classes, from stamp-making to different craft techniques like foiling or embossing. Why don't you »stamp your art« and design your own Christmas cards this year instead of sending out shop-bought ones?

Address 12 Bury Place, WC1A 2JL, Tel. +44(0)8458737005,
custom.bladerubberstamps.co.uk, stamps@bladerubber.co.uk | Public Transport Central,
Piccadilly Line, Stop Holborn | Opening Hours Mon–Sat 10.30am–6pm, Sun
11.30am–4.30pm | Tip Visit the Cartoon Museum (35 Little Russell Street). Here you
can find British cartoons and comics dating from the 18th century to the present day.

14   Bookartbookshop

Beware of the book!

The small red corner shop is not your ordinary bookshop. Behind the red door with its curved peephole there lies a whole world of unexpected books. Bookartbookshop sells artists' books and small press publications. They often have only five copies of a book; some screen-printed, hand-painted books even only exist in a single copy. The shop focuses on illustrated, textured, typographed and sculptural books, meaning that each book you open here holds a surprise. You can find books with forks sewn to their front covers and intricate pop-up books where art and text are so entwined that it's difficult to say where one begins and the other ends. There are interesting and somewhat strange stories like the crayfish that invades London; hand-sewn books, handwritten books; and even some that talk to you: »You are not dreaming, you are reading a book!«

The shop was founded by Tanya Peixoto in 2002. She was already involved in the subject of artists' books as she had edited the »Artists' Book Yearbook« for several years. At an event she proposed there should be a bookshop for artists' books and Alastair Brotchie of Atlas Press offered her the opportunity to set up Bookartbookshop. Another thing that is different about this bookshop is its close connection to the authors. Some of them drop by frequently to see whether copies of their books have sold and artists, many of them local, come in to offer their books.

Tanya also organises discussions, meetings and exhibitions; the window display is changed regularly to feature different artists. There are also private views, where you can meet the artist over a glass of wine. The shop not only count book and art lovers among their customers but also university libraries, because in times of eBooks acquiring unique artists' books makes their collections unique.

But not all books in the shop are harmless. Some of them have to come with a warning – like the book that uses a real rat trap as its opening and closing mechanism!

Address 17 Pitfield Street, N1 6HB, Tel. +442076081333, www.bookartbookshop.com,
t.pei@btinternet.com | Public Transport Northern Line, Stop Old Street | Opening Hours
Weds–Fri 1pm–7pm, Sat 12pm–6pm | Tip Nightjar (129 City Road) is a cocktail bar and
old-fashioned speakeasy with good live music and amazing drinks.

15 British Standard

Kitchen cupboards without frills

Have you always admired Shaker-style kitchens? Do you think the worktops and cupboards in a kitchen should be of high quality, but can't afford to pay a fortune? Are you interested in sustainably sourced furniture? Are you happy to plan your kitchen and put the units together yourself? If all this applies to you, pay a visit to British Standard's showroom at Hoxton Square, where you will find good quality kitchen cupboards and worktops at affordable prices.

The cupboard façades are made from poplar and the doors have solid brass hinges. The worktops are available in iroko, oak or sycamore wood. British Standard's website contains a detailed description of the process of measuring, designing, ordering, collecting and fitting your kitchen. Go ahead, why not create your own dream kitchen?

This is actually what Katie Fontana, the co-founder of the business, did herself. She and Tony Niblock bought a longhouse in Suffolk, and Katie designed the kitchen based on early Georgian models. It was so beautiful that everybody who saw it wanted one too! So they turned it into a showroom and founded Plain English, a joinery company for kitchen cupboards, which became known for its high quality and great design.

As beautiful as Plain English kitchens are, because they are bespoke and handmade, they come with a price and not a lot of people are able to afford them. Interestingly enough, Prince Charles played a pivotal role in solving this problem: Plain English collaborated with the Prince's Foundation on a project and the Prince asked Katie how to make an affordable high-quality kitchen. It didn't seem possible, but Katie rose to the challenge and designed »no frills« kitchen cupboards that could be bought online without a design, delivery or fitting service – so the same quality as Plain English could be offered at a much lower price. British Standard was born!

Address 41 Hoxton Square, N1 6PB, Tel. +44(0)2078707688,
britishstandardcupboards.co.uk, info@britishstandardcupboards.co.uk | **Public Transport**
Northern Line, Stop Old Street | **Opening Hours** Mon – Sat 10am – 5pm | **Tip** Play table
football and watch live football at football-themed Bar Kick (127 Shoreditch High Street).

16 _ Brodie & Middleton and Russell & Chapple

Two in one

What do you need in a theatre apart from actors? Paints and canvases, of course! Two different businesses share the premises in Drury Lane, both catering to the theatres nearby. Brodie & Middleton was established in 1840. It sells theatrical paints, brushes, scenic paints and stage make-up. Do you want your clothes to look dirty? Then buy the special effects spray »Dirty Down« – you can choose between a khaki, nicotine yellow or mould effect! The can warns »for professional use only«, so you had better not try this at home on your best suit!

Russell & Chapple is the older of the two businesses. It was founded in 1770 and specialises in canvases, supplying theatres, artists and colleges like the Slade, the Royal Academy School or Central Saint Martins with fine art, scenic and digital canvases. The high-quality Belgium linen, which is best for artists' canvases, is made exclusively for Russell & Chapple. But there are many other uses for their canvases, such as curtains for theatres, scenic backdrops, boat covers or aprons. The wooden stretchers to build the frames for paintings are made here as well and can go as large as three metres. Once the team at the shop had to stretch canvases for The National Gallery in the museum itself, because the frames were so big they couldn't get them through the door!

The shop was owned by Miss Chapple, an old lady in her nineties. She had no relatives and when she died, she left her business to her old manager, her old accountant and her new manager. They found it difficult to manage and decided to sell it on to Nicholas Walt, who merged the two shops into one. Although they are still separate businesses, Russell & Chapple and Brodie & Middleton are closely related – and to make things even more complicated, they also share a close link with the pigment specialist L. Cornellissen because Nicholas Walt owns all three shops.

| Dk. grey 103 | Y/orange 201 | 15ml Water Make-Up | | |

| Lt. Blue 302 | Blue 303 | Blue/azure 304 | Green 401 | Sea green 402 |

| Bt. Red 501 | Pink 502 | Orange 503 | Bordeaux 504 | Dk. Red 505 |

Address 68 Drury Lane, WC2B 5SP, Tel. +44(0)2078367521, www.russellandchapple.co.uk, info@randc.net | Public Transport Piccadilly Line, Stop Covent Garden | Opening Hours Mon–Fri 9am–5.30pm | Tip The Theatre Royal Drury Lane (Catherine Street) was already founded in 1663. It's still worth going there, especially to the spectacular family shows.

| Turquoise 742 | Green 745 | Pink 752 | Dk. Pink 753 | Red/brown 757 |

17___The Button Queen
Button etiquette

The Button Queen stocks a stunning range of antique and modern buttons, but it's not a haberdashery. Buttons take centre stage here. They not only serve to fasten garments; they are works of art and collectors' items in their own right. The shop stocks beautiful 18th-century hand-tooled silver buttons, Victorian cut pearl buttons for waistcoats, 1910 casein buttons (made from milk), 1940s buttons made of stamped wood and many more besides: over 900,000 buttons altogether! New buttons are bought with an eye to their collectability, like the official buttons of the Royal Diamond Jubilee.

But not every button can be used for every purpose, explains Martyn Frith, button expert and owner of the shop: »When Princess Diana was first married, she put some equerry royal household buttons on one of her garments and was told off.« Clearly a breach of button etiquette!

Buttons can also be of historical interest. Often people will bring in a family button box representing four generations. People have kept the buttons even though the garments don't exist anymore. When clothes were mangled, buttons had to be removed and sewn back on afterwards.

Martyn, who runs the shop together with Isabel Frith, is an inexhaustible source of button history and knowledge, although at first he didn't intend to go into the business at all. It started with Martyn's mother Toni, who was nicknamed »queen of all the buttons« when she sold buttons over 60 years ago at London antiques markets. Peter Finch, a friend and actor, suggested the name for her shop and it became the registered business title in the 1960s.

Martyn describes his mother as a veritable »force of nature«. She didn't suffer fools gladly and it happened several times that she threw people who asked stupid questions about buttons out of the shop. Maybe she was right, because after all: a button is not just a button!

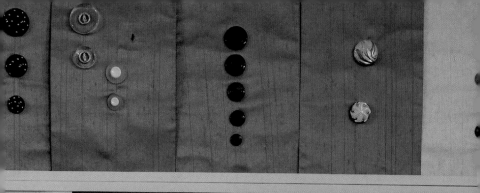

Address 76 Marylebone Lane, W1U 2PR, Tel. +44(0)2079351505,
www.thebuttonqueen.co.uk, information@thebuttonqueen.co.uk | **Public Transport**
Central, Jubilee Line, Stop Bond Street | **Opening Hours** Mon–Fri 10am–5.30pm, Sat
10am–3pm | **Tip** What about a lunchtime concert at Wigmore Hall (36 Wigmore Street),
a Victorian concert venue?

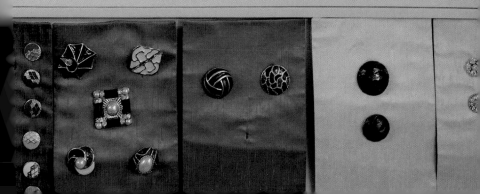

18 Candle Makers Supplies
Candles for Prince Charles

Tucked away in a small courtyard is a veritable treasure trove of all things waxy. Ann Collins manages the business side of the shop, while her partner David Constable takes care of the mail orders and makes candles. They have run Candle Makers Supplies together since 1969. It all started one Christmas when they lit some candles, shared a bottle of wine, looked at the bottle and said: »Wouldn't it be nice to have a candle in that shape?« They carried out a lot of research, finally found the base products they needed and started making candles. They then decided to set up a business, selling candle making materials, which is what they still do today.

The shop caters for other crafts as well, such as silk painting and batik. It supplies schools, charities, and a lot of candle makers. Here at Candle Makers Supplies you will find paraffin wax, applique wax sheets and moulds made from plastic, rubber or glass in all sizes and shapes. Especially popular are moulds for animal heads and edible looking fruits, for festive Christmas trees and snowmen, skulls and numbers or even tantric lovers. Of course you can also purchase wicks and dyes, candle perfumes and paints.

The shop not only stocks everything for producing candles; it even has the materials for making your own moulds – although this is probably more of an option for the advanced candle maker. As a beginner you can start with one of their candle making kits: the good thing is that if something goes wrong, you can just throw your candle back in the melting pot and start again! Maybe you would like to join one of the regular candle making classes in the shop?

Candle Makers Supplies also do bespoke candles for weddings, events and theatrical productions. For Prince Charles, they made tall thin candles to use at his table and were granted a royal warrant as candle suppliers. Might his Royal Highness also be persuaded to become a candle maker?

Make
your own candles
the easy way with a

CANDLE MAKERS SUPPLIES
CANDLEKIT

Twice as much wax as most other kits

Address behind 102–104 Shepherds Bush Road (entrance in Batoum Gardens), W6 7PD, Tel. +44(0)2076024031, mail@candlemakers.co.uk, www.candlemakers.co.uk | Public Transport Circle, Hammersmith Line, Stop Goldhawk Road | Opening Hours Mon–Fri 10.30am–6pm, Sat 10.30am–5.30pm | Tip There is a 1920s themed tearoom (Betty Blythe, 73 Blythe Road) nearby where you can enjoy your afternoon tea.

LOOK! contains more wax, wicks and dyes than it took to make these thirteen candles

With step-by-step easy to follow instructions by David Constable

The 'Original' and still the Best!

19 Choccywoccydoodah
Chocolate Wonderland

Entering Choccywoccydoodah is a bit like following the white rabbit down the rabbithole: all of a sudden you find yourself in a weird and wonderful land of extraordinary chocolate cakes! Towers of white chocolate with angels, canna lilies and butterflies compete with colourful crazy tea party cakes populated by balloons, monkeys and little monsters. You can choose between a Mona Lisa and a skull cake with the inscription »Til death do us part« or have a fairytale-inspired cake, complete with chocolate mirrors and evil queens. Or what about an enormous white chocolate stag? There appears to be no limit to what the chocolate artists working here can come up with.

It all started in 1994 when two ladies, both called Christine, inherited a small café in Brighton. When they wanted to expand their space to a next-door shop, the council only granted permission for a retail business. Overnight they baked a lot of cakes, which all sold out by 3pm the next day. From that day onwards the business has gone from strength to strength, thanks to the unique pairing of Christine and Christine. One Christine is the creative mastermind who invents her own secret recipes for sculpting chocolate; the other Christine takes care of the business side and keeps them grounded. Today they have their own TV program and in August 2013 the London Flagship store opened in Fouberts Place near Oxford Circus.

Shop on the ground floor for truffles, chunky bars, popcorn slabs, bambis, dogs, frogs and buddhas. The cakes are either available as finished products or you can place a bespoke order. Choccywoccy-doodah's cakes are moist and densely layered with different truffles: white, champagne, dark, cappuccino or praline.

Taste them in the first floor café before making your choice! And if you want to indulge even more, why not have a chocolate feast with your friends in the secret room on the second floor and share the experience of this Chocolate Wonderland?

Address 30–32 Fouberts Place, W1F 7PS, Tel. +44(0)2077349713, www.choccywoccydoodah.com, london@choccywoccydoodah.com | Public Transport Bakerloo, Victoria Line, Stop Oxford Circus | Opening Hours Mon–Sat 10am–7pm, Sun 12pm–6pm | Tip Visit Liberty, a department store famous for selling luxury goods. Did you know they used the wood of two ships when they built the store in 1924?

20 Christina's Boxes

What's in a box?

There's something about beautiful old wooden boxes that just keeps you wondering about them. You want to touch their satiny surfaces, run your fingers over their inlay work, open them and discover their secrets, and if you do … you might just find a surprise! Perhaps someone kept their love letters or childhood treasures in them – or even better, they might have a secret compartment!

Christina Tattum was always interested in boxes, and when she was made redundant from her job as graphic designer she decided to follow this passion. She began to buy and sell antique boxes 20 years ago and today has the biggest collection in London, housed in a small shop in Camden Passage in Islington. The little store is only open for two days a week and Christina uses the rest of the week to hunt for new stock. At first she was interested in writing boxes, then diversified into tea caddies, love boxes, jewellery boxes, sewing boxes, knife boxes and spice boxes. She also sells fans, trays and objects associated with boxes, such as inkwells, letter scales and the occasional writing desk.

The items date from about 1790 through to Edwardian times. You could say that the writing box was the Georgian and Edwardian equivalent of a laptop – people would take their box with them when they went away for the weekend so they could write their letters. The boxes in the shop are more than mere functional objects: they are also works of art in themselves. Christina's stock ranges from intricate Victorian papier-mâché sewing boxes to Regency boxes with pencil work in the lid made of rosewood or tea caddies with brass decorations. Depending on the piece's age and quality of work, prices can start at 50 pounds and go up to 500–600 pounds. Wouldn't it be nice to be like the American gentleman who once came to the shop to buy a whole load of them to decorate his library! A box is always mysterious, containing a wealth of possibilities. What would you like to put in it?

Address 8 Camden Passage, N1 8ED, Tel. +44(0)7780961663, www.christinatattumantiqueboxes.com, christinatattum@btinternet.com | Public Transport Northern Line, Stop Angel | Opening Hours Weds, Sat 10am–4pm and by appointment | Tip Have coffee and try the apple cake in the Austrian café Kipferl (20 Camden Passage).

21 _ The Christmas Shop
Christmas every day

Hay's Galleria is an old warehouse with an associated wharf that was redeveloped in the 1980s. Here you can find The Christmas Shop, which has been selling baubles, crackers, tinsel, paper chains, nativity sets and tree-top angels as well as Christmas cards since 1988.

Owner David Thompson and his wife Elaine went on holiday to America many years ago and saw flourishing Christmas shops there. As they had sold their previous business and were looking for something to do next, Christmas decorations seemed a nice thing to sell. Obviously this is a seasonal business. In the first months of the year, they also stock gifts and cards for Valentine's and Mother's Day. From July onwards, Christmas decorations pick up and it goes crazy from the end of October, with peak trade in the first two weeks in December. The glass decorations come from a German company and include items such as dinosaurs, pianos, suitcases, boxes of popcorn, stacks of books and beer glasses. According to David, decorations now tend to be less obviously related to Christmas: »Anything that looks nice goes on the tree.« He stocks nativity sets from Italy, decorations and figures from America and a whole London-themed collection: crowns, beefeaters, taxis, telephone boxes, Big Ben, Queen Elizabeth or Henry VIII ... there's no limit. Just imagine your own London-themed Christmas tree! The traditional English tree decorations are tinsel, baubles and paper chains, even though Christmas trees were a German invention, made popular by Prince Albert.

A Londoner named Tom Smith invented Christmas crackers, which are also sold in the shop, in 1847. Christmas decorations follow fashions that change every year, but David admits that he's more of a collector and just adds to his decorations whenever he finds one that he likes. So does he ever get tired of Christmas, having it every day? »Once it comes it's still special because it's family, but we have to decorate our Christmas tree in November.«

Address Hay's Galleria, 55A Tooley Street, SE1 2QN, Tel. +44(0)2073781998, www.thechristmasshop.co.uk, christmasshop@btconnect.com | Public Transport Jubilee, Northern Line, Stop London Bridge | Opening Hours Mon–Fri 8.30am–6pm, Sat 10am–6pm | Tip Walk along the Thames and find the Golden Hind II (1 Pickfords Wharf), a reproduction of Sir Francis Drake's ship!

22   Clerkenwell Screws

One nutcase and seven screwballs

They hold everything together and are all around us. Usually we don't notice them because they're hidden, but when one of them is loose it's no good at all. What are they? Screws! That's what you get at Clerkenwell Screws, alongside many other types of fasteners and fixings: nuts and bolts or tools like hex keys and drill bits.

Screws are available in all finishes, from steel, brass, chrome and nickel to nylon. When you enter the shop, you will be greeted by the manager Mr. Shah or one of his colleagues standing behind the counter – no one else is allowed to go behind the counter into the »inner sanctum« of screws. Among the 15,000 different types of nuts, bolts and screws, they will find the one that is right for you. Are you interested in model engineering and want to build or repair a model? They stock screws and bolts 0.89 mm big! Or if you need very light screws, buy some made of nylon.

The team of six working here are not easily caught out and whether you need five or 5000 screws makes no difference to them. It takes at least one year of training to get to know all the different bits and pieces they sell. Most of the employees have been working here for many years, like Mr. Shah who started to work at Clerkenwell Screws in 1997. In the beginning he had no special affinity to screws, but »once you are involved it gets interesting again and finally it becomes second nature.«

Nowadays most of the screws are metric, but Clerkenwell Screws has a whole room full of imperial screws, that is, screws with American or English measurements. They often get orders from German vintage motorcycle or car collectors who don't want to spoil the look of their old British motor with metric screws. If you're still desperately looking for your lost screw, remember that »one nutcase and seven screwballs« – as they call themselves – would love to help solve your problems!

Address 109 Clerkenwell Road, EC1R 5BY, Tel. +44(0)2074056504/1215, clerkenwellscrews.com, info@clerkenwellscrews.com | **Public Transport** Central Line, Stop Chancery Lane | **Opening Hours** Mon–Fri 8am–5.15pm, Sat 9am–14.45pm | **Tip** Visit St Peter's Italian Church (136 Clerkenwell Road) to get a feel of Italy in the middle of London.

23___The Cloth Shop
Addicted to fabrics

Are you one of those people who can't walk past a bolt of cloth without stroking it? Are you irresistibly drawn to old French linen? Do Irish cashmere blankets turn you on? If this is the case, then don't miss the Cloth Shop on Portobello Road!

On Fridays and Saturdays you can take a short break here from the crowds flowing up and down Portobello Market, and cloth lovers will find everything they need to feed their addiction. You can admire old linen grain sacks, Paisley scarves, colourful Liberty prints, Khadi cottons or antique Indian quilts, but you are also allowed to touch the cashmere blankets and discover their haptic quality. The stock includes old buttons, lace and embroidered ribbons and beautiful cushions made from Indian Kantha fabrics.

When you have finally finished admiring and comparing all the different fabrics and decided on a few metres of Khadi Cotton, staff members Alex, Sam and Henry are so knowledgeable and helpful that you'll be tempted to buy more – maybe a few linen towels or buttons – or rather a Durham Comfy Quilt? Why is it so difficult to decide?

Sam Harley, together with Alex Adams, has managed the shop for many years. It always was their philosophy only to buy what they liked themselves. Henry, Sam's son, has inherited his passion for beautiful fabrics. During their holidays, father and son go on »fabric hunts« all over the world to find unusual textiles. They bring back amazing cloths from their journeys, like East European linen and goat hair cart covers or embroidered Indian ribbons. As Henry grew up between bolts of fabric and has worked in the shop for a few years now, he knows nearly as much as Sam does. He can tell you about the production of English tie silk or the different qualities of linen sold in the shop. Henry, Alex and Sam also recommend upholsterers and tailors, cut off samples for you and send fabrics abroad. What better place to become a fabric addict?

Address 290 Portobello Road, W10 5TE, Tel. +44(0)2089686001, www.theclothshop.net, theclothshop@gmail.com | Public Transport Circle, District, Hammersmith, City Line, Stop Ladbroke Grove | Opening Hours Mon–Sat 10am–6pm, Sun 11am–5pm | Tip On Saturdays and Sundays you'll find good vintage and fashion deals on Portobello Green Market (beneath the Westway flyover).

24 Colin Narbeth & Son
The art of collecting

Under the roof of Colin Narbeth & Son you'll find dealers in different collectors' items. If you collect coins, medals or paper money, this little shop in the »collector's row« Cecil Court is the place to go.

To the non-collector all those objects will look pretty much the same, and he or she might wonder what it is that makes collecting such a fascinating and all-consuming occupation, often turning collectors into dealers. To understand, you have to step into the world of collectors. Stephen Wheeler deals in military medals and declarations from all over the world. Like many dealers he started out as a collector, fascinated by the history attached to each individual medal. Medals from mainland Europe for example come with papers that document their history, whereas English medals have the names of the recipients engraved into them. You can choose between a medal awarded at Waterloo, medals from the 1866 Prussian-Austrian war to medals from the First and Second World Wars. The actions these were awarded for have influenced the outcome of wars and the course of history. Equally fascinating coins document historical and political events.

Philipp Cohen, the proprietor of Coin Heritage, has been in the trade for over 35 years. He started collecting coins as a child – before the introduction of the decimal system in Britain – when you could still find coins in circulation that were struck in 1860. »The value of a coin,« he explains, »is determined by several different factors like rarity, condition, but also by supply and demand.« The rarest coin he ever came across was a 1952 half crown – only a few of them were struck and were put into circulation by accident. Since the time he had it in his hands, it has risen in value by a factor of 30. Both dealers recommend only to collect what you can afford and really interests you. What would you like to start your collection with: a medal awarded by Ludwig II of Bavaria or a 2500-year-old coin from Pakistan?

Address 20 Cecil Court, Charing Cross Road, WC2N 4HE, Tel. +44(0)2073796975, colin-narbeth.com, narbeth@btconnect.com | **Public Transport** Northern, Piccadilly Line, Stop Leicester Square | **Opening Hours** Mon–Fri 10.30am–5.30pm, Sat 10.30–5pm | **Tip** Not far from here is Brydges Place, the smallest alleyway in London.

25 Contemporary Ceramics Centre

To become a good potter

After exploring Neolithic, Sumerian, Egyptian and Greek pottery in the British Museum, why not continue your journey with a foray into contemporary ceramics? This gallery-cum-shop is located directly opposite the Museum. Its calm atmosphere and spaciousness invite you to stay as long as you need to look at all the exhibits – and there's a lot to see: every artist has her/his own shelf or space, and there is another room in the back with changing exhibitions showing select ceramicists.

The mix in the shop is eclectic, including a wide range of styles and pottery techniques. Smoothly glazed marbled bowls stand side by side with rough volcanic-looking, organically shaped vessels. Your eyes alight upon a bowl made of many staring faces, adjacent to five sea urchins clinging together to form a teapot. Wafer-thin black stem cups are positioned beside vessels that depict everyday household items like mops or graters. Two ceramic hares fight above a pig and a horse, opposite some pots that could well be part of the Egyptian or Etruscan collection at the British Museum. In the Museum you can admire the makers' craft, but here you can actually buy every single piece of ceramic art!

Marta Donaghey, who has worked at the Centre for twenty-five years, explains that it all began with a group of potters who wanted to exchange glazes. In 1958 they formed the Craftsmen Potters Association and a year later opened a shop, which moved a few times and later was renamed the Contemporary Ceramics Centre. Today the gallery is able to choose from work produced by over 350 members. A committee of ten to twelve makers decides what is going to be exhibited. They go strictly for the highest standard – personal taste doesn't come into it. Some of the exhibitors have been members for 50 years while others are newcomers, but most of the potters here are over thirty – simply because that is how long it takes to reach this standard of pottery!

Address 63 Great Russell Street, WC1B 3BF, Tel. +44(0)2072429644, www.cpaceramics.com, info@cpaceramics.com | Public Transport Central, Piccadilly Line, Stop Holborn | Opening Hours Mon–Sat 10.30am–6pm | Tip If you still have energy left, visit Sir John Soane's Museum (13 Lincoln's Inn Fields).

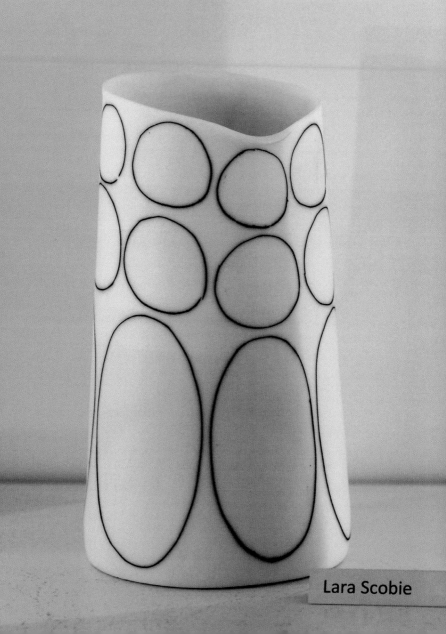

Lara Scobie

26 CorkVille

In Portugal's cork forests

Just imagine endless forests of ancient cork oaks with their shining red trunks: this is where Maria Ferreira grew up. Cork is something natural for her – something she used to touch and play with when she was a child. She grew up in Portugal and her family worked in the cork business.

Some years ago, cork stoppers for wine bottles started to be replaced with metal or plastic stoppers, which led to a downturn in Portugal's cork industry. It was only natural for Maria to think of other uses for cork and to open a little shop selling cork products in Lisbon. In 2012 the economic crisis forced her to close the shop and she moved to Britain. She was still convinced of the beauty and versatility of the material, which led her to open CorkVille in Greenwich Market in June 2013.

Here she sells handbags, backpacks, shoes, hats, accessories, notebooks, umbrellas and home products, all made from 100 percent cork. Did you know that cork is as durable and supple as leather, water resistant, lightweight, tolerant to extreme heat, stain and scratch resistant, sustainable and floats? Cork is simply an amazing material! A cork oak can live about 200 years and the bark is harvested for the first time when the tree is about 30 years old. It can be removed every nine years.

So anybody who wants to grow cork is in for the long run. The cork oak is the only tree that has a renewable bark. Maria sources her products from Portuguese artisans and designs the handbags herself. Once you know all this, you will see cork with different eyes and take a closer look at its beautiful structure. You will be very tempted to buy a pair of beautiful cork ballerinas or sandals – or maybe a colourful handbag or wallet? A cork hat will definitely protect you from rain, but the shop's crowning glory is the cork umbrella. Just imagine walking with it through a shower in Portugal's cork forests!

Address 17 Greenwich Market, SE10 9HZ, Tel. +44(0)2036098230, http://corkville.co.uk |
Public Transport DLR towards Lewisham, Stop Cutty Sark | Opening Hours Tues–Sun
10am–6pm | Tip Visit the Cutty Sark, an old tea and wool clipper that later became a
training ship for cadets.

27 David Mellor

Eat with Pride

It all started in 1953 when David Mellor designed his first range of cutlery at the Royal College of Art. It was called Pride and became a classic. In the 1960s, David set up a silversmithing workshop in Sheffield and received commissions for one-off pieces like the table silver for British embassies.

He also determined the appearance of British streets to a major degree by redesigning the national traffic light system and street furniture such as lampposts and post boxes. In 1969 he opened a shop in Sloane Square called David Mellor Ironmonger, where he sold nails, doorknobs and hammers alongside cutlery and silver. It turned out that nails and hammers didn't pay the rent and so the shop was turned into a cookshop, which it still is today.

Today, David's son Corin is the creative director of David Mellor Design. He also cherry-picks designs of other makers for the shop: be it a traditional Swedish teapot, Walter Gropius TAC Porcelain by Rosenthal, or Dave Regester's hand-turned wooden bowls. Corin is fascinated by the process of making things. Like his father, he not only designs beautiful cutlery but also carries out special commissions, like the benches for Chatsworth House or an advent wreath for Sheffield Cathedral. Corin is also responsible for the interiors of the design museum, café and shop on the site of the cutlery factory in Sheffield.

His cutlery and tableware designs are simple and elegant, like the translucent Fine Bone China or the Black Handle kitchen knives. His British Standard Mugs with their bright 1950s colours will cheer you up when you have your first cuppa of the morning. Like his father's designs, Corin's have the potential to become timeless classics. Pride is still the bestselling cutlery at David Mellor's, available in stainless steel, silver plate or sterling silver. You can still eat with Pride!

Address 4 Sloane Square, SW1W 8EE, Tel. +44(0)2077304259, www.davidmellordesign.com, ssq@davidmellordesign.co.uk | Public Transport Circle, District Line, Stop Sloane Square | Opening Hours Mon–Sat 9.30am–6pm, Sun 11am–5pm | Tip The Saatchi Gallery (Duke of York's HQ, King's Road) shows and sells contemporary art, from Damien Hirst to new African or South American artists.

DAVID MELLOR CUTLERY

28___David Penton & Son

Good Old-School Hardware

Good old-school hardware: that's what it says on David Penton & Son's business card, and that's what it is! Hardware shops are local institutions, but unfortunately they are disappearing from British high streets. What do they sell? Everything – or at least everything you need in and around the house. Cliff Vigors is Penton's shop manager. He has worked here for 15 years and feels very passionate about the shop. He particularly loves creating the window displays: the window's centerpieces are a beautiful 1920s clock with »Penton« written on its face, and »George«, a cardboard dummy and advert for wall plugs, who by now has become the most famous man in Marylebone. When he was taken down for cleaning one time, there were several complaints!

On a typical Saturday morning the shop is busy with builders and tradesmen, but from 11am onwards the locals come in. Some of them return every Saturday. »There's a real village feel to it,« says Cliff, »and a lot of the customers are women. Every woman loves a hardware shop.« Small wonder: what woman could resist feather dusters, a mushroom brush or a wooden clothes airer? And there are so many more things to discover here: from brushes, brooms and cleaning products to keys and locks, tools, screws, hooks, doorknobs, watering cans and hot water bottles, toilet seats and drainage covers, the shop is filled to overflowing with an overwhelming selection of useful items.

Besides offering customers advice, Cliff can also tell you a lot about the shop's history. It was founded in 1841 as a leather grindery, making saddles, boots and shoes for the disabled patients treated in nearby Harley Street. The old sewing machine that was used for this work can still be seen in the window. Later, the grindery became a hardware and ironmonger's store. While the owners changed several times, Penton's stayed and now is one of the few surviving hardware shops in Central London. Not only locals shop at Penton's: larger businesses like John Lewis's or Claridge's also have accounts here. Everyone loves a good old-school hardware shop around the corner!

Address 64 Marylebone Lane, W1U 2PE, Tel. +44(0)2079356962,
www.pentonshardware.co.uk, info@pentonshardware.co.uk | Public Transport Central, Jubilee Line, Stop Bond Street | Opening Hours Mon-Fri 8.30am–5pm, Sat
9.30am–5pm | Tip The nearby Wallace Collection (Hertford House, Manchester Square)
displays wonderful French 18th-century painting, furniture and porcelain.

29 Denton Antiques
Ablaze with light

Hundreds of sparkling crystal and glass chandeliers that capture every bit of light are set against the dark blue walls in Denton Antiques, a family business in Kensington Church Street, run today by the fourth generation of the Denton family. It all started with the formidable Mrs Crick, who opened a bookshop here around 1900. By chance she came into possession of a chandelier, which she then sold in her shop with great success. She decided to branch out and started selling chandeliers as well as books. One of her daughters married the antiques dealer Mr Denton, who had a shop in Marylebone High Street. In 1983 both shops were finally united – the differently named shop windows still show the two interlinked families – at 156 Kensington Church Street.

Major changes were made in 1998 when the family opened out the basement and leveled the shop with the street, gaining enough height to hang all the beautiful antique chandeliers. Today they sell mainly English and French designs from between 1780 and 1920. There is also a workshop in the back where the light fixtures are repaired and a few reproductions are made. Denton chandeliers hang in important public buildings like St Paul's Cathedral or the Royal Albert Hall, where »Promenaders« – people who visit the Proms – collected money to buy a large chandelier and 16 wall lights from Denton. But the shop also gets many private customers: Middle Eastern ladies who often like coloured chandeliers, or Russians who prefer Russian chandeliers. Most of them have very big rooms to hang them – a service Denton also provides, traveling as far as Cairo or Beijing to install the chandeliers. They also sell beautiful smaller designs, from lanterns and wall lights to candelabras.

The Dentons have always understood the importance of light: when victory was celebrated at the end of the Second World War they lit candles in the shop window, setting it ablaze with light after six years of darkness!

Address 156 Kensington Church Street, W8 4BN, Tel. +44(0)2072295866,
www.denton-antiques.co.uk, info@denton-antiques.co.uk | Public Transport Central, Circle,
District Line, Stop Notting Hill Gate | Opening Hours Mon–Fri 9.30am–5.30pm,
Sat–Sun 9am–5pm | Tip The Diana Memorial Playground (The Broad Walk) in Kensing-
ton Gardens is a treat for children with its big wooden pirate ship, teepees and a beach.

30 D. M. Buttonholes

Buttonholes for James Bond

Have you ever thought of buying a buttonhole? No? After you've talked to David from D. M. Buttonholes, you will ask yourself why you didn't think of it much earlier.

The shop was founded nearly 100 years ago by David's great-aunt. After that it was owned by David's father, and today David is the owner and manager of the business. He grew up in the shop and already covered buttons with fabric when he was a child. He knows the big impressive sewing machines resembling green metallic monsters inside out. One of them only produces buttonholes for shirts, another works solely with black or blue thread. Others again only make eyelets in different sizes or press studs. There's a machine for textile-covered buttons and one to sew the buttons on. They also produce differently sized and shaped buttonholes. You can have round buttonholes, buttonholes for reverses or with eyelets; and fish-tail buttonholes.

The shop is tucked away in a basement in the heart of Soho, and whoever comes here usually knows exactly what he or she is looking for. A lot of fashion students are among David's customers, but they also include renowned fashion designers like the late Alexander McQueen, who used to sit in a corner of the shop and wait for his buttonholes. Businesses on Savile Row commission the buttonholes for their shirts and costume designers ask him to make the openings with matching buttons for film or theatre costumes – for example, he did the buttonholes for the latest James Bond film. Individual customers order fabric-covered buttons with matching holes for their wedding dresses here. David never knows who will find his or her way into his basement next and enjoys the challenges and variety of his job. Once he had to sew 900 eyelets on a garment.

No matter if you want one hole or ten holes, you will get them for the same price. So how many would you like on your jacket?

Address 11b Wardour Mews, D'Arblay Street, W1F 8AN Tel. +44(0)207437-8897, www.dmbuttons.co.uk, dmbuttons@aol.com | **Public Transport** Bakerloo, Central, Victoria Line, Stop Oxford Circus | **Opening Hours** Mon–Fri 7.30am–3pm | **Tip** Walk to Soho Square. Sit down on a bench or on the lawn and watch people from all over the world.

31 D. R. Harris

Oranges and Lemons …

How did the 18th- or 19th-century gentleman freshen up? At that time, not even the rich bathed on a daily basis. A gentleman would thus attempt to avoid unpleasant smells by using perfumes or colognes distributed generously all over his body. It turned out that citrusy colognes fragranced with oranges and lemons were best suited to mask pungent body odours.

Harris's Apothecary, founded by Daniel Rotely (D. R.) and Henry Harris in 1790, quickly gained an excellent reputation among the gentry for its colognes and perfumes. Its location in St. James's was convenient for serving customers from gentlemen's clubs and St James's Court. Nowadays body odours are somewhat less of a problem, but the colognes and perfumes produced and sold by D. R. Harris remain highly popular.

Still owned by the Harris family, the business has successfully blended tradition and innovation for the last two centuries. Today it sells soaps, perfumes, colognes, as well as skincare and shaving products – and not only to English gentlemen, but to customers from all over the world. Colognes from D. R. Harris have become known as traditionally English scents, and some of them were already formulated in Victorian times. Alison Moore, who manages the shop, considers developing new lines of cosmetics one of her job's most exciting aspects. The latest line, »Windsor«, was created to mark the Queen's Diamond Jubilee. Its fragrance is based on a blend of grapefruit, vetiver and black pepper.

As an independent, fully functioning pharmacy, D. R. Harris also serves the local community, an aspect taken very seriously by everyone who works there. The shop holds two royal warrants for their services. At the moment, the apothecary has moved to Bury Street while the premises in St. James's are being redeveloped. After 18 months it will return to the premises in St. James's with their beautiful original interiors and the fragrance of oranges and lemons.

Address 35 Bury Street, SW1Y 6AY, Tel. +44(0)2079303915, www.drharris.co.uk, sales@drharris.co.uk | Public Transport Jubilee, Piccadilly, Victoria Line, Stop Green Park | Opening Hours Mon–Fri 8.30am–6pm, Sat 9.30am–5pm | Tip Pamper yourself and go for a cocktail in the Ritz Hotel (150 Piccadilly)!

32 Duke of Uke

Why don't you?

It's a small instrument, but don't underestimate it! George Harrison was a big fan. Elvis Presley played it in Blue Hawaii, as did Marilyn Monroe famously in Some Like It Hot. Ten years ago it had fallen out of fashion, but has since been rediscovered and become very popular again. You've probably guessed it – Duke of Uke in Shoreditch sells ukuleles.

Owner Matthew Reynolds anticipated the resurgence of this small member of the guitar family and opened his shop in 2005. The ukulele is a small-scale four-string guitar and most likely originates in Portugal, where it was called a machete. Sailors took the instrument with them for entertainment on their long trips and it eventually found its way to Hawaii, where it was redesigned and became the national Hawaiian instrument. Ukulele roughly translates as »jumping flea«, although according to the last Hawaiian queen it means »the gift that came here«. The instrument spread from Hawaii to the USA and had its heyday there in the 1920s and 1930s.

Shop manager Kieran explains that they sell four sizes of ukulele: soprano, which is the smallest with its typical, slightly mad ukulele sound, concert, tenor and baritone. Buying a ukulele is not terribly expensive. An instrument suitable for a beginner can be purchased for relatively little, although depending on the wood the price can go quite high. The most expensive material is koa, a Hawaiian wood. Because it's small and much easier to learn than a guitar, the ukulele has become the most widely taught children's instrument in schools. Brilliant ukulele players like Jake Shimabukuro and the Ukulele Orchestra of Great Britain have also contributed to its revival. There is another advantage: unlike other instruments, the ukulele doesn't seem to evoke fierce competition. Ukulelists play happily together in a group. So if George, Elvis and Marilyn played it, why don't you? Book Duke of Uke's ten-week ukulele course!

Address 88 Cheshire Street, E2 6EH, Tel. +44(0)2035839728, www.dukeofuke.co.uk, info@dukeofuke.co.uk | Public Transport Circle, District, Hammersmith Line, Stop Whitechapel | Opening Hours Tues–Fri 12pm–7pm, Sat–Sun 12pm–6pm | Tip Visit nearby Spitalfields City Farm (Buxton Street). They have lovely pigs, goats, donkeys and other animals, do wildlife and vegetable gardening, all supported by the local community.

33 Embassy Electrical Supplies

Electric olive oil

What does olive oil have in common with light bulbs, cables and fuses? Nothing, you would think – but Mehmet Murat, the owner of Embassy Electrical Supplies, proves the opposite. He sells all of these items in his shop in Clerkenwell, and there is an interesting story to this.

Mehmet is from Cyprus and moved to the UK in 1955. He trained as an electrician and opened the electrical supplies shop in 1974. Meanwhile, back in Cyprus, his father – who sold the British army the donkeys that they used in Egypt – bought a plot of land near Mehmet's native village of Louroujina and planted an olive grove there. After his father's death Mehmet took over, imported all the olive oil to the UK and bottled it himself.

In 2005 he purchased another olive grove in Turkey and in a good year can now produce up to 5,000 litres of olive oil, which he sells under the name »murat du carta«. The olives are handpicked in the traditional way. Most of the pickers are women, who climb the trees with great dexterity. Immediately after harvesting the olives are taken to the mill and pressed without any additives. Mehmet's wife and brother look after the groves and so he has been able to branch out into lemons, pomegranate molasses, sweet paprika, candied walnuts and chili flakes. His family also forages for wild herbs, which he sells in his shop as well.

The oil is regarded as the »best olive oil in England« and is popular with restaurants and private customers alike. Mehmet has actually become quite famous and has been interviewed many times by newspapers and magazines. Olive oil and electrical goods might be an unusual combination, but for him it makes sense to have one business instead of two. When asked which of the two he prefers, he says: »The electrical goods are still my bread-and-butter income, but my heart is in the olives, because these I produce and the electrical goods I only sell.«

Address 76 Compton Street, EC1V 0BN, Tel. +44(0)2072514721, www.mroliveoil.com, embassyelectric@aol.com | Public Transport Circle, Hammersmith, Metropolitan Line, Stop Farringdon | Opening Hours Mon–Fri 9am–5pm, Sat 9am–2pm | Tip Would you like to learn about the area? Go to Islington Museum (245 St John Street)!

34__FARM Collective
Simple Food

Are you hungry and looking for a place to have lunch, breakfast or just a snack? FARM Collective offers an alternative to the ubiquitous chain cafés and eateries populating British high streets. Here you will get »honest British food« sourced from small producers.

Co-owners Dominic Kamara and Craig Wills are old school friends. They wanted to do something together and first had the idea of opening a pie and mash shop. After visiting farmer's markets and tasting all the lovely British food they offered, they realised that city workers weren't able to get food like this during the week. A concept was developed with the aim to get good products from farms around England directly into the city.

Helped by friends, they started to make sandwiches in a small kitchen and sent them out to the financial district by bicycle. This was a big success and they were able to open the shop in Cowcross Street in 2009, followed by two other shops in 2012 and 2013. They not only sell food, but also donate ten percent of their profits to a charity that helps inner-city kids and child carers to take holidays in the countryside.

In Cowcross Street they do salads and sandwiches, all freshly made on the premises. The bread comes from Flower Power City Bakery, an organic London bakery. Meat is sourced from Smithfield Market in close connection with the suppliers, and even the tea comes from England – it is grown on a tea estate in Cornwall. Dominic and Craig look very closely at the products' prices, because they want to sell the best quality at an affordable price. One secret behind their success is to keep the food traditional and offer things like cottage pie or fish finger sandwiches. When he was a child, Dominic's grandmother in Cornwall used to make cottage pie for him. He wants to recreate this homely feeling with the food they're making. He's obviously on to something, as the people who come here like simple food!

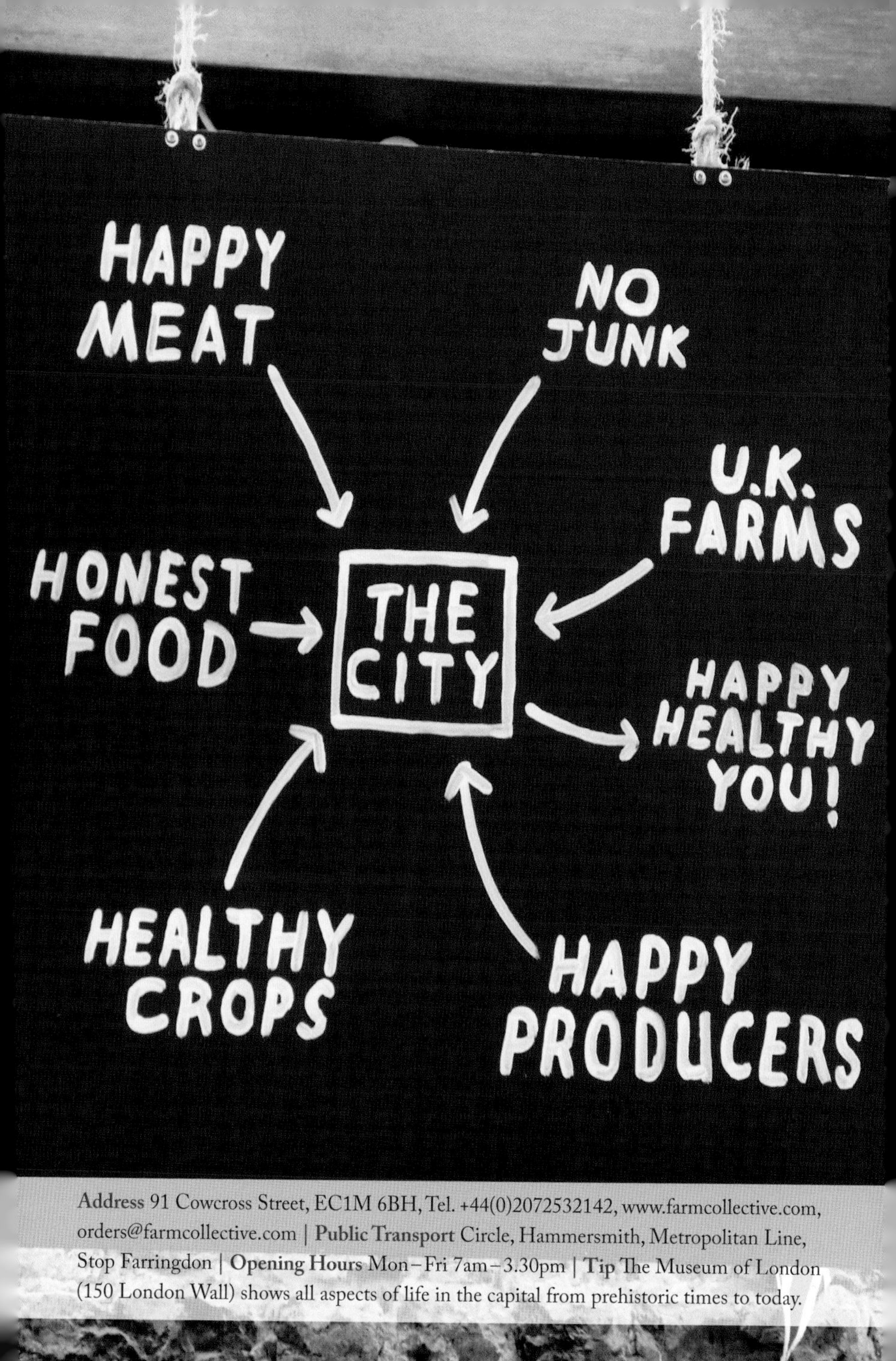

HAPPY MEAT

NO JUNK

U.K. FARMS

HONEST FOOD → THE CITY ← U.K. FARMS

→ HAPPY HEALTHY YOU!

HEALTHY CROPS

HAPPY PRODUCERS

Address 91 Cowcross Street, EC1M 6BH, Tel. +44(0)2072532142, www.farmcollective.com, orders@farmcollective.com | Public Transport Circle, Hammersmith, Metropolitan Line, Stop Farringdon | Opening Hours Mon–Fri 7am–3.30pm | Tip The Museum of London (150 London Wall) shows all aspects of life in the capital from prehistoric times to today.

35_Farm:shop Dalston
Let the fish grow your salad!

Are you interested in growing your own food, but live in a city? Then have a look at the world's first urban farming hub in Dalston. Farm:shop Dalston has a café, a small aquaponic fish farm, an indoor allotment, a chicken coop and a polytunnel. The building belongs to Hackney Council and used to be a women's shelter.

After that it stood vacant for two years before the council held a competition to find a new use for it. Andrew Merrit, Paul Smyth and Sam Henderson from the design agency Something & Son won and opened Farm:shop in 2011. The design team had a lot of help in realising the shop: The aquaponic system was donated and installed by Aquaponics UK, the wood came from leftovers of the Olympic Park and a lot of volunteers helped and are still helping to run the café and do other work around the place.

But what is aquaponics actually? It is a system that combines aquaculture – in this case a tropical fish called tilapia – and hydroculture – growing plants in water. Patrizio, one of the volunteers, used to run a blueberry farm in Argentina. All the blueberries were exported to the USA and Canada. He came here to look at different forms of farming that don't involve as many food miles. As aquaponics is his hobby, he knows a lot about it. »The fish produce ammonia, which is toxic for them in high concentration. Bacteria transform the ammonia into nitrates, which feed the plants. You basically feed the plants from the fish waste.« They grow salad and herbs on floating rafts that sit directly on the water. The salad is then used for sandwiches in the café.

The other products sold here are locally sourced as well. The coffee is roasted at Glimpson & Son in Hackney and a girl called Soffie cooks really good pitta chips for them. They haven't found a local cow yet for their milk, so please come forward if you have any suggestions! Until then, enjoy their excellent salad grown by fish!

Address 20 Dalston Lane, E83AZ, Tel. +44(0)2034905124, www.farmlondon.weebly.com, lisa.ommanney@somethingandson.com | Public Transport London Overground towards Stratford, Stop Dalston Kingsland | Opening Hours Mon–Sun 11am–5pm | Tip Visit nearby Dalston Eastern Curve Garden (13 Dalston Lane). It's a lovely garden with a very active community space and activities for children.

36__ The Gallery
Bass guitar with sex appeal

Where do you buy or repair your bass guitar in London? The best place to go is The Gallery in Royal College Street in Camden. A short distance from the hustle and bustle of Camden Market, you will find a huge range of instruments, amps and accessories in this shop. The stock is amazing, ranging from beautiful American vintage Fenders to eight-string instruments. You can also commission your own custom-built bass guitar. The »Sei bass« workshop in the basement both repairs basses and makes them from scratch.

The shop's owner, Martin Petersen, came to London in 1987 to become a bass player. However, it turned out that guitar making was a better option for him and he opened the shop in 1993 after completing a course in Modern Fretted Guitar Making at the London College of Furniture. The concept was to sell bespoke basses as well as instruments by other small independent makers. His customers include many professionals: bass players who have performed with The Who, Annie Lennox, Joan Armatrading or Take That. But Martin states that »professionals usually have less money than people with a day job, who are able to afford several guitars or maybe even collect them«!

Bass guitars are made from hardwood such as ebony, rosewood or bird's eye maple. Depending on which type of wood is used, the tonal quality of the instrument varies. If you use ebony you will get a much harder sound than from guitars made of rosewood, which has a lower density and produces a softer, warmer tone. Except for the shape, which is Sei bass's signature, things like string spacing, scaling or pick-ups can be altered specific to the customer's requirements. Some clients are very meticulous and come to look at their instrument on a weekly basis while it is being built. So what is the special relationship between a bass guitarist and his or her instrument? Recent studies have discovered that women find men much more attractive if they are holding a guitar – and female bass players have even more sex appeal!

Address 142 Royal College Street, NW1 0TA, Tel. +44(0)2072675458, www.thebassgallery.com | **Public Transport** Northern Line, Stop Camden Town | **Opening Hours** Mon–Thurs 10.30am–5pm, Fri 10.30am–5.30pm, Sat 11am–5pm | **Tip** Camden Lock Market is a real must for teenagers, but there is something for all other age groups here too. Try the exciting array of street food!

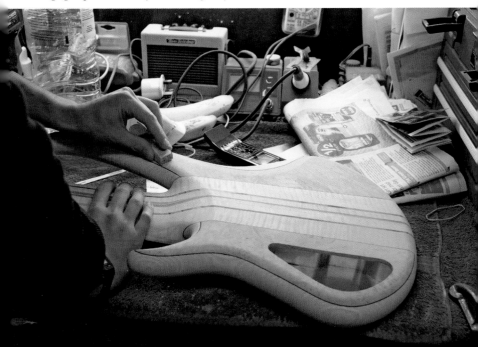

37 Gallery 196
Things that make you smile

The first thing you notice when you enter the shop are the colours: bright and bold oranges, pinks, reds and blues. You really should go here on a grey, rainy day – you will be cheered up immediately! Susan Richardson, the owner of the business, says that many customers come here when they feel the need for a bit of colour in their lives. Sometimes they tell her: »Sorry, I'm not buying anything today but I just felt like I wanted to come and look!«

Susan sells craft items and textiles from all over the world, especially India and Asia. She opened the corner shop on the ground floor of her own house in 2010/11. It is a wonderful addition to the lively Primrose Hill neighbourhood, which is full of cafés and small independent businesses. Susan has always been fascinated by craft. She is a textile designer and weaver by trade and worked all over India for many years, later becoming a buyer for companies like Graham and Greene. She then decided that she was too old to work for someone else and wanted to push boundaries further. Opening the shop is part of her personal mission to bring a bit of the exuberance of India back to the UK and to support craftspeople in different countries.

Today she has personal contact to many of the craftsmen whose products she sells. Often things are made especially for her, such as the mirror masks made by a 90-year-old artist. She stocks Banjara textiles from Central India, Kantha cloth made from used textiles, Turkish book holders, toys from Sri Lanka and Moroccan salad spoons hand-carved from lemon wood. From Jaipur, Susan imports block prints; she has pajamas made there as well. Another of the shop's distinctive features are the beautiful vintage and new reverse glass paintings.

Susan thinks that humour has an important part in crafts, for example in the funny soap dishes formed like cats or goats from the Faiyum in Egypt. Susan likes things that make her – and her customers – smile!

Address Regent's Park Road, NW1 8XP, Tel. +44(0)2077220438, www.gallery196.com, info@gallery196.com | Public Transport Northern Line, Stop Chalk Farm | Opening Hours Tues–Sat 10.30am–6pm, Sun 11.30am–5.30pm | Tip Primrose Hill affords some of the best views in London!

38__ Gay's The Word

The first and only

The bookshop Gay's the word is named after a musical by Ivor Novello. Founded in 1979, it was the first bookshop in Britain to cater exclusively to the gay, lesbian and transgender communities, and today it is the only queer bookshop left in the UK. It stocks a great range of gay, lesbian and trans literature, poetry, crime, travel and erotic fiction. With its mixture of new and antiquarian books you'll be sure to find something for every taste, whether it's queer historical, political or philosophical works, such as political books about Islamic homosexuality or homosexual desire in revolutionary Russia, a biography of Ludwig II or Carson McCullers's »The Ballad of the Sad Café.«

Gay's The Word has always been more than a bookshop. Although it was founded by one person, a lot of people bought into the shop and supported the idea of a gay and lesbian bookshop. The shop now has evolved into a real centre for the community. Besides readings and book events, lesbian discussion groups hold their meetings here, parents come to seek advice on how to handle the coming-out of their teenage children, or families with gay partners look for children's books that mirror their modern-day family. Jim MacSweeney, who runs the shop with a co-worker, describes its unique atmosphere: »That's the interesting thing about working here. You get people from 16 to 90, all shapes and sizes and it feels like a community.«

Jim has been working here since 1989. He really enjoys interacting with customers and loves talking to them about books they've read and plays they've seen or discussing the situation of gays and lesbians in, for example, India and China. He wants to share his passion for the books he loves and thinks it is very important to have a friendly space like this in London, which can be a cold place at times. Small shops like Gay's The Word are constantly threatened by rising rents – it would be a huge pity to lose the first and only gay and lesbian bookshop in the UK.

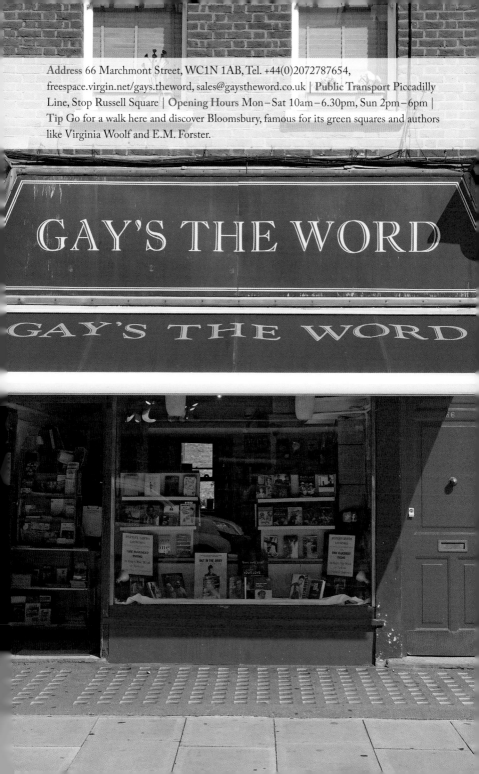

Address 66 Marchmont Street, WC1N 1AB, Tel. +44(0)2072787654,
freespace.virgin.net/gays.theword, sales@gaystheword.co.uk | Public Transport Piccadilly
Line, Stop Russell Square | Opening Hours Mon–Sat 10am–6.30pm, Sun 2pm–6pm |
Tip Go for a walk here and discover Bloomsbury, famous for its green squares and authors
like Virginia Woolf and E.M. Forster.

39 __ Gillian Anderson Price
An antidote to globalisation

Brook Street in exclusive Mayfair is dominated by big brands. In nearby Bond Street you'll find all the big fashion labels, but you can also find the same shops in Paris, Rome, Berlin and New York and buy exactly the same things as in London.

Gillian Anderson Price, sandwiched in between all these big stores, is different. It is a unique shop and the things sold here you can't buy anywhere else. Gillian, the shop's owner, has been in antiques nearly all her life, learning about the trade from a very young age because her parents had an antiques shop themselves. She sells vintage homeware, jewellery and curiosities, but it is difficult to pinpoint what she specialises in.

The shop offers everything from jewellery, 1960s Gucci handbags, silk top hats, bulb light signs, gnomes and old jelly molds to Victorian planters. The underlying principle is to buy and sell only things she loves. One of her areas of interest is suffragette jewellery. To support their cause, suffragettes wore jewellery in the colours green for hope, white for purity and purple or violet for dignity, sometimes also interpreted as »Give women the vote«. All of the jewellery was made around 1910 and Gillian mainly sells costume jewellery, which she buys from a lady who has a big collection of suffragette jewellery and sends her a parcel from time to time.

She also stocks amazing bulb lights that form big letters or signs, which are actually the only new things she sells. They are created by the artist and craftsman John Morissey and can be custom-made at no extra cost. All these things are special and unique presents. »It's not about how much a gift costs, but about finding the right gift for the right person.« Her clients, mostly people who love quirky vintage things, often ask her to source something specific for them, be it a handbag, brooch or even an old Playboy magazine! She sometimes feels like an »antidote to globalisation«.

Address 16 Brook Street, W1S 1BE, Tel. +44(0)2074081016, www.gillianandersonprice.com, info@gillianandersonprice.com | Public Transport Central, Jubilee Line, Stop Bond Street | Opening Hours Mon–Sat 10am–6pm | Tip Handel has his museum in Brook Street, but did you know that another famous musician, Jimi Hendrix, lived next door (23 Brook Street) to Handel, albeit a few years later?

40___Gosh!

From children's story books to art form

Gosh! resides in Berwick Street in a vibrant mixed neighbourhood, where you can find everything from sex shops to fabric stores. It opened in 1986 as a back issue comic shop in Bloomsbury, where it remained for twenty-five years, only moving to Berwick Street a few years ago. Joshua Palmano, the owner and founder of Gosh!, enjoys all the bustle and creative talent around him here in Soho. A lot of the people who buy comics here, work in the film industry, design or PR. Even customers he thought he had lost with his move, such as parents with small children, are still coming to the shop.

As he started dealing with comics at the age of twelve and opened his shop when he was 19, Joshua's experience and knowledge of his field is extensive. He talks about how the market has »developed enormously in the last 30 years. Then it was largely American comics and comics for kids. Now it is adults creating comics for adults.« Artists like Joe Sacco changed the medium in the early Nineties. Sacco inspired the journalistic side of comics, writing about the Middle East and the war in former Yugoslavia. Marjane Satrapi's Persepolis, the autobiographical story of her childhood in Iran, is another very influential graphic novel that also made biographical comics very popular.

When Gosh! first opened, it had only one shelf of graphic novels. Now the shop is full of them. Over the last ten years, the Internet and cheap publishing have opened the market up even further. Small publishers are cropping up and filling the gaps. Comics are used as teaching devices in schools, they are present in public libraries, and they attract children who normally don't like to read. Gosh! also promotes new talent with a weekly workshop/discussion group for aspiring and working comic artists. From Tom Gould's clean lines and simple shapes to the reinvented Superhero novels, comics are an art form of their own with a wide array of languages and styles – why not visit Gosh! and see for yourself?

Address 1 Berwick Street, W1F 0DR, Tel. +44(0)2076361011, www.goshlondon.com, info@goshlondon.com | Public Transport Central, Northern Line, Stop Tottenham Court Road | Opening Hours daily 10.30am–7pm | Tip Berwick Street Market (Mon-Sat) sells mainly fruit, vegetables and flowers. There are some food stalls and household items as well.

41__Grosvenor Prints

Discover Print Paradise

Once you've found this well-hidden gem with its bright yellow façade, you won't want to leave again! Visitors can spend hours and hours browsing through its enormous collection of prints from the 16th to the 20th century.

It seems as if the shop has been here for ages, but in fact it only opened eight years ago in this location, although owner Nigel Talbot first started dealing in prints in 1976. He founded a shop in Covent Garden in 1980 at a time when there were a lot of prints around, buying over 100,000 of them over a six-month period from a dealer who provided him with a lot of help and financial advice. Prior to this Nigel was a print collector and, like all collectors, also did a bit of dealing. Today he has one of the largest selections of antique prints in London and spends most of his time driving around the country going to auctions as well as buying from other dealers in Western Europe.

His customers come from all over the world and a lot of them buy solely via his large website. About 40% of sales are shipped outside the United Kingdom. It sometimes happens that someone from the other side of the world is looking for a specific portrait; if Nigel is able to help, reactions are like: »I've been looking for a portrait of this man for thirty years. You've made my life better!« Nigel stocks about 30,000 portraits – they are one of his favourite subjects – but you will find just about everything else here, from animals and plants to political or battle prints. Grosvenor Prints stocks rare or special prints, such as the beautiful luminous Georgian glass prints whose technique remains a secret because nobody knows how the special heat treatment they were made with worked.

Before the Internet and TV, prints often served a political function and very popular motifs were reprinted or even re-engraved several times, such as the Indian Chief, sitting under a tree lost in thought. Keep browsing and you might find a treasure of your own here in print paradise!

Address 19 Shelton Street, WC2H 9JN, Tel. +44 (0)2078361979, www.grosvenorprints.com, grosvenorprints@btinternet.com | **Public Transport** Piccadilly Line, Stop Covent Garden | **Opening Hours** Mon–Fri 10–6pm, Sat 11–4pm | **Tip** There are a few famous restaurants nearby, like the L'Atelier De Joel Robuchon (13–15 West Street) or the Ivy (1–5 West Street).

42_ The Hive Honey Shop

More bees on the planet

20,000 bees fly in and out of the Hive Honey Shop, and you can watch them at their busy lives behind a tall glass wall. The shop's owner James Hamill – who has been chosen as London Beekeeper of the Year 2013 – has beekeeping in his blood. He has kept bees himself since he was 5 years old and there have been beekeepers in his family for the last three generations.

When he first opened the shop in 1992, he found it difficult to get people to understand that the shop sold only honey and honey products. So James installed one of the largest observation beehives ever built in his shop! The Hive Honey Shop owns over 100 beehives and sells its own honey. For James, honey is an amazing product. He compares it to fine wines because it can have so many different colours, flavours and textures, depending on which plants the bees have visited and at what time of year.

The beekeeper has his beehives at different sites around the country, taking them to floral areas he knows will yield a specific type of honey. He thus obtains varieties such as jewelweed, heather or sainfoin honey - to name only a few of the honey types. James's German wife Uta has a background in cooking and develops gourmet honeys with added flavours like ginger, raspberry or cinnamon. The shop also sells honey produced by small individual beekeepers from all over the world.

Among the shop's other products are cosmetics, lotions and potions made by James's family based on their own recipes and using ingredients harvested from their beehives. The anti-bacterial properties of honey, royal jelly and propolis have been known for a long time: propolis was even found in Ancient Egyptian tombs. The Hive Honey Shop sells an ointment based on a recipe developed 90 years ago that can help with eczema and psoriasis. To encourage as many people as possible to keep bees, James also sells live bees and gives beekeeping courses, because »the more people we have looking after bees the more bees we have on the planet«.

Address 93 Northcote Road, SW11 6PL, Tel. +44(0)2079246233, www.thehivehoneyshop.co.uk, info@thehivehoneyshop.co.uk | **Public Transport** London Overground towards Clapham Junction, Stop Clapham Junction | **Opening Hours** Mon, Tues, Thurs, Fri, Sat 10am–1pm & 2pm–5pm, Weds 2pm–5pm | **Tip** Follow the bees to Wandsworth Common, which today is a park with ponds, meadows and trees. In medieval times commons had the right to graze their animals here.

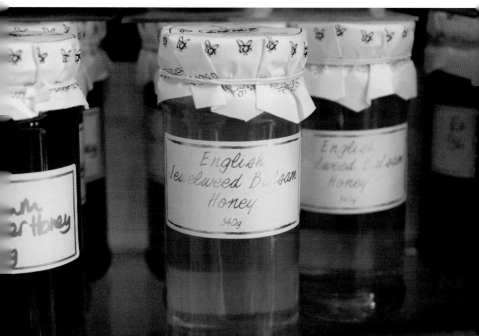

43__Hostem

Craft, construction and quality

Founded in 2010 at 41–43 Redchurch Street, Hostem is one of the most avant-garde fashion boutiques in London. Shoreditch has become a centre for the creative industry and a luxury shopping destination, and Hostem has established a reputation as one of the most exciting menswear shops in London. It is a must for any man even remotely interested in design, not only because of the fashion but also because of the shop's interior, which is the work of JAMESPLUMB, a design team consisting of Hannah Plumb and James Russel.

Found objects, reclaimed materials and a sense of scene and space come together to form one of the most interesting shop interiors in London, where even less style-conscious men can feel confident enough to buy clothes by designers like Ann Demeulemeester, Damir Doma or Haider Ackermann. The bespoke area in the basement is another of the shop's bonuses. Here you can have shoes made by Sebastian Tarek that will take three fittings and six months to finish; a suit made by Joe Casely-Hayford, a well-known British fashion designer; a bespoke suitcase by Globetrotter; or you could commission an interior or a piece of furniture with JAMESPLUMB.

In 2013 Hostem branched out into women's wear, remodeling the two top floors of the building and dedicating them to female attire. These floors are also designed by JAMESPLUMB, but the aesthetics and atmosphere are completely different here. Whereas the men's floors are in warm wood tones, the parquet here is steel and the walls are cool white polished plaster. The department stocks designers like Yohji Yamamoto, Amy Revier or Meadham Kirchhoff. Even though these two spaces are completely unalike, the underlying attention to detail is visible in both areas. Founder James Brown says that they didn't want to be typecast, so they used a different approach for the women's wear. When asked what he thinks is most important to him, he answers: »Craft, construction and quality.«

44 iMakr

3D Selfie

Have you ever used a 3D printer to design and print your own object? If so, you are one of only a few among the world's seven billion people. »But this will change,« says Sylvain Preumont, the founder of iMakr on Clerkenwell Road. »3D printing will be the next big thing to change our lives after the Internet. It is not about if, it is about when.«

Sylvain is a technology entrepreneur with years of experience. He wanted to make 3D printing, which at the moment is still mostly used by large companies, accessible to individual consumers and give them a chance to see and use 3D printing technology. He opened iMakr, the world's largest 3D printing store, in 2012. iMakr stocks a range of different printers at affordable prices, as well as materials, 3D-printed objects and scanners.

So what do you need for 3D printing and how is it done? You need a printer and a 3D printable model, which you can create using computer-aided design software (CAD) or a 3D scanner. The shop also has an archive of free downloadable designs on their website. A lot of 3D printers in the shop use filaments that melt. The most common are two plastics: ABS and PLA. But there are others as well: use laywood, consisting of 40 percent recycled wood with a binding polymer, if you want your object to look and smell like wood. Laybrick looks like sandstone and is a mix of milled chalk and harmless co-polyesters. Other materials include nylon, rubber and conductive filaments. You can create your own toys, jewellery or gadgets, design glasses or even shoes, make models, print and replace a broken spare part for your hoover, design a fancy case for your phone or print your own lampshade – the possibilities are endless! You can learn how to print all these things at iMakr by booking one of their training sessions or taking part in a workshop or demonstration. If you are still in doubt that 3D printing is the future, get a »mini-you«: a 3D miniature of yourself in full colour!

Address 79 Clerkenwell Road, EC1R 5AR, Tel. +44(0)2074043828, www.imakr.com, info@imakr.com | Public Transport Circle, Hammersmith, Metropolitan Line, Stop Farringdon | Opening Hours Mon–Fri 10am–8pm, Sat 10am–7pm | Tip Not far from here is Sadler's Wells Theatre (Rosebery Avenue), where you can see extraordinary dance performances.

45___Intaglio Printmaker
Get your tools

What is a biffer, a shader tool or a mezzotint rocker? They all are etching tools used for intaglio: printmaking techniques where the incised areas hold the ink. Intaglio was used by many major artists, including Albrecht Dürer, Francisco Goya and Pablo Picasso.

If you're looking for any of the etching tools described you'll find them at Intaglio Printmaker, a specialist for printmaking materials in South London. The shop stocks an unparalleled range of the printmaking materials you'll need if you want to do etching, engraving, relief printing, screen printing or lithography. It was founded in 1981 and has a strong Australian connection. The Australian owner brought over Karyn White, an artist who studied printmaking in Melbourne, to manage the shop. Christine Munton, a British lady who worked as a financial controller for a firm of stockbrokers, was engaged to do the accounting and look after the business's financial side.

In 1988 Christine and Karyn decided to take the plunge and buy the shop from the original owners. Although it is a small company, Intaglio sources and delivers printmaking materials worldwide. Some of the tools, like dabbers, are made in the shop, while others such as the big presses are custom-made for Intaglio to their specifications. Many schools, colleges and universities as well as artists order their materials from them.

The six or seven people working in the shop are all artists themselves and specialise in different areas of printmaking. One is Peter, whose area of expertise is screen printing. He explains that screen printing works like a stencil: »You paint a stencil or stick a paper on the screen, which consists of a fine mash through which the paint is squished and everything that is covered up is blocked.« Today, screen printing is widely used in the fashion industry because you can easily print on textiles or garments – basically on any flat surface. What are you waiting for? Get your tools and start printing!

Address 9 Playhouse Court, 62 Southwark Bridge Road, SE1 0AT, Tel. +44(0)2079282633, www.intaglioprintmaker.com, info@intaglioprintmaker.com | **Public Transport** Jubilee Line, Stop Southwark | **Opening Hours** Mon–Fri 10am–6pm, Sat 11am–4pm | **Tip** Walk to Borough Market (8 Southwark Street), London's most renowned food market.

46__International Magic

Bring on the magic!

Martin McMillan's family is able to look back on over 50 years of magic. Martin's father Ron, who was an award-winning magician himself, founded the family business around 1960. When Ron started his family he gave up touring the world and wanted to do something that allowed him to stay with his wife and children – so he set up International Magic.

Today, his children Martin and Georgia run the shop. Martin grew up with magic and started to work here straight after leaving school. He modestly admits that he knows a few tricks but hesitates to call himself a magician. Great magicians like David Copperfield, Derren Brown or Dynamo not only work very hard and study a lot but also have a strong relationship with their audience: »There is a distinction between magicians and trick-doers. A trick-doer performs the tricks but won't understand how magic works on people.« Martin and his family are also the organisers of the annual magic convention in London. For a week, magicians from all over the world give lectures, compete with one another and perform for public audiences. Sometimes even Martin is surprised by some of the tricks that are shown!

The shop supplies magic tricks on all levels to tourists, amateurs and professionals. But they won't sell a difficult magic trick to a beginner, because he or she just hasn't studied enough magic to understand or perform it. Everyone who works here can advise people about the level and the kind of magic they want to perform. You will use a different trick close up than for a big stage; you can do street magic, children's magic or mentalism, which is mind reading. What about a card or coin trick? The staff here not only advise aspiring magicians on what to buy, they also go through the tricks with them. Sometimes a customer comes back to show them what he or she has learned – and buys the next trick. International Magic definitely still have some tricks up their sleeves!

Address 89 Clerkenwell Road, EC1R 5BX, Tel. +44(0)2074057324,
www.internationalmagic.com, admin@internationalmagic.com | **Public Transport**
Circle, Hammersmith, Metropolitan Line, Stop Farringdon | **Opening Hours** Mon–Fri
11.30am–6pm, Sat 11.30am–4pm | **Tip** The Museum of the Order of Saint John (St
John's Street) tells the fascinating story of the Order of Saint John.

47_ J&B The Shop
Stitching and Enameling

If you are looking for a special gift for someone with a poet's soul, look no further. In J&B you'll find something both poetic and personal, and it will most likely have a touch of the Welsh countryside about it, because that is where the two co-owners Jessie Chorley and Buddug Humphreys are from. Both come from Snowdonia, North Wales, and met on an art foundation course in Bangor.

After moving to London, Jessie studied Textiles while Buddug specialised in Jewellery and Silversmithing. During their university years they dreamed of opening a small shop and in 2005 set up a stall at Broadway Market. This was a kind of test run for J&B, which they finally opened in 2010 in Columbia Road. Their concept is that they only sell things they make themselves, complemented by the occasional vintage piece. Buddug does enamelwork. She uses a kiln, putting several layers of enamel on metal and scratching into them. The results are poetic and unique plates, Welsh love spoons – a spoon you give your loved one in Wales – or jewellery, often with Welsh poems or anthems scratched into it. Buddug also creates a lot of personalised pieces for weddings or other special occasions.

Jessie makes textiles and stationery, but her work is better described as »painting with needles«. Materials and her direct surroundings inspire her: she collects old books and vintage clothing and draws, embroiders and sews on them. She makes bags from old curtains, scrapbooks or journals from old books, designs cards and personal books for weddings and also creates stamps and a range of wrapping paper. Jessie gives workshops where you can learn to use different materials and techniques. Buddug and Jessie get a lot of customers from Japan, America and Wales, who also buy on their website.

The shop is only open four days a week; the rest of the time they need for stitching and enameling in their studio, because making things is what they love most – and this is what gives their pieces their poetic and personal touch.

Address 158a Columbia Road, E2 7RG, Tel. +44(0)7708921550, www.jandbtheshoplondon.bigcartel.com, jessiechorley@hotmail.com | Public Transport Central Line, Stop Bethnal Green | Opening Hours Thurs–Fri 12pm–6pm, Sat 12pm–4.30pm, Sun 9am–4.30pm | Tip Not far from here is the V&A Museum of Childhood (Cambridge Heath Road). Great fun for children and adults!

48__Jane Bourvis
Something old …

Stepping into Jane Bourvis's shop is like entering a dream of old lace, silk and tulle. Located in Golborne Road near Portobello Market, it produces and sells wedding dresses made from antique lace and textiles. The shop also sells bridal shoes, vintage accessories and beautiful antique jewellery.

The owner, Jane Bourvis, has a background in menswear fashion. For many years she worked for a Japanese company, but lost her job in the 90s when the economic crisis hit Japan. This proved a blessing in disguise for brides wanting to wear beautiful old lace for their wedding! Jane opened the shop in 1997, at first selling gifts and small items with the wedding dress production evolving only slowly. Jane's first commission was an evening dress for a singer; this proved so successful that more and more people wanted her to make dresses for them. Motivated by her love of old textiles, lace and vintage dresses, she then started sewing wedding dresses: in her opinion, women look simply incredible in old lace because it is so soft and falls so well. Nowadays she makes 3 – 4 lace dresses a week, mostly from old veils. One day a week is set aside to cut new dresses, which is Jane's favourite part of the work. Usually a bride will try on several half-made dresses, which are kept in the shop. If she likes one of them she can buy it and it will be fitted and finished to her specifications within about a week.

Brides love the shop and its fairy-tale atmosphere. A bride is supposed to be happy by definition, but occasionally problems can arise – especially if the bride's mother wants something different from the bride herself! But none of this matters as long as the bride turns out beautiful and happy in the end, which Jane does her utmost to ensure. For Jane, shopping is a social experience: meeting people, going out and seeing extraordinary things. This social dimension is one thing lacking on the Internet. So why not go out and find »something old« for the bride in Jane Bourvis's shop?

Address 89 Golborne Road, W10 5NL, Tel. +44(0)2089645603, www.janebourvis.co.uk, jane@bourvis.freeserve.co.uk | Public Transport Circle, Hammersmith Line, Stop Westbourne Park | Opening Hours Tues–Fri 12.30pm–6pm, Sat 10.30am–5.30pm | Tip Enjoy little Portugal and have breakfast in one of the excellent and cheap Portuguese cafés (Lisboa or O'Porto) on Golborne Road.

49 Japanese Knife Company
The cutting edge

How long does it take to learn how to make knives? A lifetime, a Japanese master would probably say, and the normal apprenticeship period is about 18 to 20 years; the best masters are all in their 70s and 80s.

Jay Patel, the director of the Japanese Knife Company, found out from personal experience that learning about Japanese knife culture takes a long time. While travelling around the world to learn how to cook, he was given a knife by a Japanese chef that changed his life. He started an apprenticeship with a blacksmith in Japan and stayed there for ten years. Seven of these ten years he spent with his teacher making knives, staying in Kyoto two more years to learn how to sharpen them and then spending another year at a fish market where he learned how to use them.

One year after returning to London he finally opened the Japanese Knife Company, the first shop in Britain dedicated to the kitchen knife. It became so popular with professional chefs and passionate amateurs that the company was able to open two further shops in London. They stock the biggest range of Japanese knives outside Japan. A lot of them are handmade by the old masters, but Jay didn't only want to sell Japanese knives; learning so much about Japanese knife culture has enabled him to create something new. He realised that Japanese and western cooks use knives differently. So he spent two weeks with individual blacksmiths in their workshops in Japan, creating knives that merged Japanese and western needs. Although every knife the company sells is functional and usually so sharp it cuts through paper, some of them are also amazingly beautiful works of art.

Another important part of knife culture is sharpening, because unfortunately no knife stays sharp forever. Not only does the Japanese Knife Company offer all the tools needed and a free re-sharpening service, they also teach you how to sharpen your knife to make sure it always stays »cutting edge«!

Address 36 Baker Street, W1U 3EU, Tel. +44(0)2074874868, www.japaneseknifecompany.com, general@jkcl.co.uk | Public Transport Bakerloo, Circle, Hammersmith, Jubilee, Metropolitan Line, Stop Baker Street | Opening Hours Mon–Sat 10.30am–6pm | Tip Sherlock Holmes fans, walk down Baker Street to number 221B!

50__JAS
The sound of the sitar

Situated in Chiltern Street in Marylebone is a very unusual shop for musical instruments. It only sells traditional Indian instruments manufactured in the company's own factory in Delhi. The owner and founding director of the business, Harjit Shah Singh, opened the shop in 1985 together with his wife Jasmeet.

Although his family was very musical – his father was a famous tabla player – he didn't set out to become a manufacturer of musical instruments. He studied engineering and commerce in India and came to Britain in 1984. He was asked to purchase four harmoniums in India for a Sikh temple in London. The ones he found were so bad he was embarrassed and started researching the craft of making traditional Indian instruments. At the time, their standard was very low compared to western handmade instruments. Harjit decided to learn everything he could about instrument making but was met with resistance from his family. He belonged to the highest caste and was not supposed to work with his hands, something only members of the lower castes would do. Against all odds he succeeded in taking a degree in instrument technology at London Guildhall University. It helped him enormously in understanding the manufacturing side of things and how instruments could be improved.

Today JAS makes and sells stringed instruments, including the dilruba, tanpura, veena and sitar as well as percussion instruments like the tabla, dhol, dholak, naal and pakhawaj or flutes, murlis and bansuris. The shop also sells books about Indian music, teaching books and DVDs. Vocal, sitar and tabla classes are offered. Over the years their instruments have become popular not only with schools and Sikh and Hindu temples in Britain; many famous Indian musicians such as Talvin Singh, Asha Bhosle and Pandit Sharda Sahai have bought their instruments at JAS. The shop has also gained a reputation among western musicians like John McLaughlin and Jimmy Page, who had his sitar repaired here.

Address 14 Chiltern Street, W1U 7PY, Tel. +44(0)2079350793, www.jas-musicals.com, info@jas-musicals.com | Public Transport Bakerloo, Circle, Hammersmith, Jubilee, Metropolitan Line, Stop Baker Street | Opening Hours Mon–Sat 10.30am–5pm, Sun by appointment | Tip You can visit concerts at The Royal Academy of Music (Marylebone Road), but you can also go to its museum filled with historic instruments and musical items, such as a Stradivari played by Marie Antoinette.

51__J. J. Fox of St James's
Cigars for Churchill

The armchair the famous British Prime Minister used to sit in and smoke is still standing in the shop. You can easily imagine that he might come back at any moment, sit down and light one of his favourite cigars from the Romeo Factory in Cuba. One of them lasts for one hour and 40 minutes, and Churchill got through six or seven a day. Besides the leather-covered chair, you will also find other Churchill memorabilia here, such as a letter in which Churchill's private secretary orders cigars for the birthday of the minister's grandson: »if you would send a box of 25 cigars of good quality, but not quite as good as the Romeo & Juliet« – which was Churchill's preferred cigar. When he bought them, the shop was still called Robert Lewis and had already existed in this place since 1787. Later they merged with J. J. Fox, another established shop for smoking supplies that had its origins in Dublin in 1891.

Today Fox stocks 131 different types, sizes and brands of cigar. They are distinguished by length, thickness and shape. There are different formats called Corona, Panatela or the Churchill format, a particularly long and thick cigar produced exclusively for the Prime Minister in Cuba. Most cigars are hand rolled. If you cut a so-called long filler cigar open, you can see it consists of three different types of tobacco leaves, bound together with a binder. It is put into a press for 20 minutes, surrounded by a fairly wet, pliable wrapper and left to dry under a curing roof for several months.

At Fox's, the cigars are stored in a room with 60–70% air humidity to prevent them drying out. There is also a smoking lounge on the first floor. Philip Sheridan, who started to work here five years ago, has a lot of experience and is convinced cigar smokers are friendly and relaxed people. »Cigar smokers are rarely in a hurry because many cigars will last for an hour or more.« In times of »slow food«, you could also enjoy a »slow smoke«!

Address 19 St James's Street, SW1A 1ES, Tel, +44(0)2079303787, www.jjfox.co.uk, freddie@jjfox.co.uk | **Public Transport** Jubilee, Piccadilly, Victoria Line, Stop Green Park | **Opening Hours** Mon–Fri 9.30am–17.45pm, Sat 9.30am–5pm | **Tip** In nearby St James's Park you'll find different kinds of waterfowl, including pelicans. Some of them are famous for sitting down next to visitors on a bench!

52 John Davies Framing

Beautifully framed

Have you ever admired a beautiful picture frame more than the picture itself? In that case, John Davies Framing is the right place for you! The shop's interiors are stunning: gilt-framed paintings of tulips originally imported from a 17th-century Dutch teahouse adorn the ceilings and original frames and reproductions cover the walls. If you wish to treat your picture to a Chippendale, Louis XIV, Cassetta, Tabernakel, Florentine, Ripple or Cabinet-style frame, they will either have it in store, find it or make it for you. The reproductions are made to order, mainly using traditional techniques, but you can also simply send in a photograph of your favourite picture and get a computer image of your painting in a historically accurate frame!

John Davies founded the company's workshops in Fakenham in 1969. They became renowned for their craftsmanship and authentic reconstructions of Dutch, Flemish and mid-European frames. Still run by its founder, today the company works with private collectors, restorers, galleries, auction houses and museums and tries to cater to their different needs. »It is possible,« says shop manager Jemma Armstrong, »that we make a frame for a Picasso painting which will be sold in an auction and two weeks later the new owner comes back to us and wants a different frame.«

Jemma, John Davies's stepdaughter, has been involved in the family business since she was 13 years old. Although her professional career took a different direction at first – she studied psychology and took a Master's degree in criminal justice, working for the probation and drug services – she later decided to return to the beautiful side of life. She enjoys all the different aspects of the business, from gilding and restoring to Photoshop. To her, what makes her job special is that not only is she able to see wonderful paintings that are not shown in public because they are in the hands of a private collector – she is also able to frame them beautifully.

Address 8 Bury Street, SW1Y 6AB, Tel. +44(0)2079307977, www.johndaviesframing.com, john@johndaviesframing.com | Public Transport Jubilee, Piccadilly, Victoria Line, Stop Green Park | Opening Hours Mon–Fri 9am–5.30 pm | Tip Go to Christie's (8 King Street)! In the salerooms, property from upcoming sales is displayed open to the public and free of charge.

53 John Lobb
Shoes for Life

In exclusive St James's Street, which runs from Piccadilly to St James's Palace, you'll find shops dedicated to craftsmanship and high quality bespoke British fashion. One of the most distinguished of these is John Lobb, with a brown and golden façade that epitomises elegance and traditional values. At Lobb's, shoes and boots are handmade to measure the same way they were over 100 years ago when the shop was founded in 1849. From George Bernhard Shaw to Frank Sinatra, Andy Warhol and Harold MacMillan: they all had their footwear made here. Enter the shop and cast a reverent glance at the beautifully made shoes, displayed in glass cases like jewels.

However, the history of the business is more colourful than you might think given its distinguished appearance. John Lobb, a farmer's son from Cornwall, injured his foot in an accident and was unable to carry on farming, so was apprenticed to a local boot maker. The ambitious young man tried in vain to gain employment in London and so went to Australia at the time of the gold rush. But instead of searching for gold, he made miners' boots with cavities in the heels to hide nuggets! After a few years he became homesick and returned to London, where he managed to make a pair of boots for the Prince of Wales. He was granted a royal warrant and his shoes won many prizes.

Later his son moved the shop to St James's, where all the gentlemen's clubs were located. Today John Hunter Lobb, the founder's great-grandson, manages the business. The family is proud of their craft and the next generation is already working in the shop. All the shoes are sewn individually by hand and each customer had his or her own pair of »lasts«, the wooden block from which the shoe is made. Lobb stores them all – 15,000 pairs by now – in case the customer wants another pair of shoes. It is not cheap to buy shoes here, but they last an entire lifetime!

Address 9 St James's Street, SW1A 1EF, Tel. +44(0)2079303664, www.johnlobbltd.co.uk, enquiries@johnlobbltd.co.uk | Public Transport Jubilee, Picca-dilly, Victoria Line, Stop Green Park, Piccadilly Circus | Opening Hours Mon–Fri 9am–17.30pm, Sat 9am–16.30pm | Tip Spencer House (27 St James's Place), the opulent London residence of Princess Diana's family, is open for guided tours on Sundays.

54_ The Junk Shop and Spreadeagle

Everything you never knew you wanted

Like Dr Who's Tardis, this shop is bigger on the inside than on the outside. Toby Moy, who owns the business, comes from a family of antiques dealers – his father Dick established it in 1954. It is one of the last remaining shops of its kind in Greenwich, which was once filled with similar places. As it is not easy to survive, Toby has divided the basement into 14 separate units and rented them out to different artists and traders. The courtyard is by no means empty either.

Here you will find rusty fireplaces, Edwardian children's beds and many other things, including a skeleton pub sign – most likely the relic of a Goth bar. Toby gets most of his stock from house clearances, something you get a sense of walking through the different areas of the shop: the two porcelain dogs might have stood on someone's mantelpiece together with the 70s radio; a broken doll was left on a broken chair next to a spinning wheel; a croquet set, a collection of teapots looking like cottages, another collection of tins from the 1920s to the 1970s; a storm lantern, a horn, a set of scales, library stairs, a captain's uniform, a collection of Stilton jars, the inside of a telephone box, a wash bowl and pitcher…basically anything and everything! Most of it may be junk for you, but could be a great find for someone else.

You can spend hours here looking at things, going on and on because just around the corner you are sure to discover something exciting! Stay long enough and you may seriously start to consider buying a collection of rusty saws or a beautiful pair of wooden crutches – but what will your family say when you come home with all this stuff? Don't panic: have a cup of tea! In the back is a lovely tearoom with mismatched porcelain and a brass samovar. Feeling better now? Now you can see it's definitely ok to buy the lovely blue jug with the Paisley pattern!

Address 9 Greenwich South Street, SE10 8NW, Tel. +44(0)2083051666, www.thejunkshopandspreadeagle.co.uk, enquiries@thejunkshopandspreadeagle.co.uk | Public Transport DLR towards Lewisham, Stop Greenwich | Opening Hours Mon–Sun 10am–6pm | Tip Walk to Greenwich Park! Besides the Royal Observatory, you'll also find a deer park, an orchard and some Roman ruins here.

55 Kristin Baybars

A miniature world

»Please knock, don't ring the bell!« says a sign on the door of the small shop in Gospel Oak, North London. Kristin Baybars shop near Gospel Oak Overground Station is not easily found because it is far away from the main shopping areas.

The dusty shop window allows you glimpses of a meticulously furnished doll's house. Take heart, knock quietly on the door, and once inside you'll feel you've entered a different world – a much smaller one! You have to move carefully because literally everywhere are toys, and most of them are very small. There's hardly the space to turn around to see a whole circus complete with tightrope walker, lion tamer and jugglers in a glass box – coming to life if you feed them with a 20 pence coin. On the shelves, miniature furniture from beds and cupboards, loos, baths and sinks to outdoor furniture and plants are displayed. A whole section is dedicated to food, crockery and cutlery. You can see what can be done with all of this if you carefully open the beautifully furnished Victorian doll's house. Another area contains things that make for happy children's birthday parties: jumping beans, bouncy balls and slinkies.

In the tiny back room, a sign announces that »Unaccompanied children will be sold into slavery.« Here you don't even dare to breathe for fear you might accidentally knock over one of the tiny market stalls filled with seasonal fruits and vegetables. A painter has left his half-finished seascape standing on an easel amongst pots of paint; a hunter is up to no good with a rifle slung over his shoulder; and 100 tiny kittens relax in front of a grocery store.

Kristin, who founded the shop over 40 years ago, comes from a family of artists but sees herself as a craftswoman. The shop feels like a museum rather than a shop. She created her miniature world to show the talent and creativity of British craftsmen. Knock quietly and you might be allowed in!

Address 7 Mansfield Road, NW3 2JD, Tel. +44(0)2072670934 | Public Transport London Overground towards Stratford, Stop Gospel Oak | Opening Hours Tues–Sat 11am–6pm | Tip Go to Hampstead Heath for a walk! If you come on a warm summer's day, you could even have a swim at the nearby Lido (South Hill Park, Hampstead Heath).

56__Labour and Wait
Timeless designs

Anyone who has not gone into raptures over household goods has never been to Labour and Wait. The shop doesn't stock decorative items: everything here has a purpose.

Labour and Wait is the brainchild of two menswear designers. When Rachel Wythe-Moran and Simon Watkins were working in the fashion industry they had to redesign every season, no matter how much potential a garment had to become a classic. This was frustrating, because they liked the idea of timeless products used by generation after generation. In France they had seen hardware shops where you could buy everything from dustpans to slippers. So they developed Labour and Wait, opening it in 2000 in Cheshire Street.

In 2010 the shop moved to Redchurch Street because more space was required. For Rachel and Simon, beauty and functionality go hand in hand; they sell both classics and future classics. A lot of the things have evolved over time and now have a form that just works – like the simple vegetable peeler. Some objects are old acquaintances people have encountered as children. Many customers come to shop and immediately remember the round Duralex glasses they had in school. The Sussex trug dates back to the 1500s and customers might have seen them dangling on their grandmother's arm while she harvested fruit or picked flowers. The lovely Welsh blankets are a mixture of old and new, inspired by old patterns but newly designed.

Several items are manufactured exclusively for Labour and Wait, such as the clear-glazed version of the humble »Brown Betty« teapot going back to the 17th century, the screwdriver made by a cabinet maker who couldn't find the right tool, or the apron that was originally designed in-house for the people working in the shop. It became so popular that they now even sell different versions of it. Rachel and Simon are constantly looking out for products that can become future classics – even if they have to design them themselves!

Address 85 Redchurch Street, E2 7DJ, Tel. +44(0)2077296253, www.labourandwait.co.uk, info@labourandwait.co.uk | **Public Transport** London Overground towards Clapham Junction, Stop Shoreditch High Street | **Opening Hours** Tues–Sun 11am–6pm | **Tip** Go shopping in Redchurch Street. Quite a few trendy fashion boutiques have moved here over the last few years!

57 L. Cornelissen & Son
Ultramarine, verdigris and vermilion

This artist's supplies shop with its wooden interiors seems like it has been here forever. Although the shop was founded in 1854 it only moved to the current premises in 1987, taking with it all the Victorian shop fittings from its previous location in Great Queen Street.

The Belgian Cornellissen family founded the business, which had had two legs: printmaking and pigments. The minerals for the pigments were ground in the shop and the colours were made to order. Over time they supplied paints and canvases to many artists, including Walter Sickert who was once visited by Mr William Toms, a long-standing Cornellissen employee.

Sickert showed him a portrait of the artist Chloe Forbes-Robertson he was painting, asking: »What do you think of it? Don't you think she is beautiful?« She had sunken eyes and a long scrawny neck, and Toms replied: »I'm sorry, Mr Sickert. I can't see any beauty there.« He then saw a form rising from the couch: it was Chloe! At that time the business had already fallen into decline. The last two Cornellissens finally sold the shop to Nicholas Walt and his partner, a Greek icon specialist. In 1987 they had to move from Great Queen Street because the building was bought by a pornographer who threatened to break their kneecaps if they didn't move out within six months!

Today Cornellissen is a bustling shop that stocks over 15,000 different items. Many of the friendly and knowledgeable employees are artists themselves. The shop boasts an extensive array of pastels, brushes, and materials for gilding, restoration and printmaking. Cornellissen still sells 120 different pigments, among them a range called early colours, often used by restorers and museums to match the original colours – and how amazing these jars of jewel-coloured pigments look against the background of the Victorian shop fittings!

Address 105 Great Russell Street, WC1B 3RY, Tel. +44(0)2076361045, www.cornelissen.com, info@cornelissen.com | Public Transport Central, Northern Line, Stop Tottenham Court Road | Opening Hours Mon – Sat 9.30am – 6pm | Tip Another well-known old family business nearby is James Smith & Sons (53 New Oxford Street), the famous umbrella shop.

58 The Linen Cupboard
Cats, tea pots and the Canterbury Cathedral

Situated near Oxford Circus with its chains and megastores, the Linen Cupboard seems like a relic from a different era. In the shop window is a display of dishtowels with cats, teapots, Canterbury Cathedral, London sights and calendars printed on them. Your mother and grandmother might have collected these towels in the 1970s, buying a new one with a calendar every year. They bring up memories of sitting in the kitchen on Sunday afternoons, with a freshly baked cake just taken out of the oven.

When you enter the shop you will find the owner, Mr Green, standing behind the counter. He opened the shop in 1969 and still manages it today. As his father had a similar shop for household linen, it seemed a natural thing for him to do. Mr Green only stocks a limited selection of goods. The shop specialises in dishcloths, bed linen, baby linen, bath towels and tableware and also stocks duvets and pillows. Mr Green will happily show you how to use roller towels: they are towels sewn into a loop, running on a wooden peg. You hang them up in the kitchen or bathroom and dry your hands with the towel. The tea towels have traditional designs, either check or white with coloured stripes on both ends. The handkerchiefs and napkins he stocks are made from Irish linen.

Apart from its 1970s charm, one of the shop's main attractions are its prices: you can buy good quality dishcloths or bath sheets for a few pounds. Asked how he manages to keep his prices so low, Mr Green explains his business philosophy. He wants to sell very high quality products at a very low price, so he sources his goods mainly from English or Irish manufacturers, and as he works alone in the shop he has no staff expenses and is able to keep his prices down. His customers love his philosophy! Anyone who has been here once comes back time and time again and recommends the shop to others. What's not to like about cats, teapots or Canterbury Cathedral? Why don't you buy a dishcloth for your grandmother?

Address 21&22 Great Castle Street, W1G 0HY, Tel. +44(0)2076294062, thelinencupboardlondon.com | **Public Transport** Bakerloo, Central, Victoria Line, Stop Oxford Circus | **Opening Hours** Mon – Fri 10am – 6pm, Sat 10am – 5pm, Sun 10am – 4pm | Tip The Royal Institute of British Architects (66 Portland Place) has a bookshop specialising in architecture, a café, a restaurant and a library.

59 __ Lock & Co. Hatters

Miss Piggy's trilby

Lock's status as the oldest hatter in the world is undisputed. It first opened its doors in 6 St James's Street in 1676. It is also one of the oldest family-owned businesses still in existence. The shop holds two royal warrants and fitted out the great and the good, including Charlie Chaplin, Winston Churchill and Admiral Nelson. The drawings for Nelson's hat can still be seen in the shop. Lock also invented the coke, better known as the bowler hat. This hat was created in 1850 for William Coke, a progressive farmer from Norfolk, and was supposed to protect gamekeepers from overhanging branches. Its hardened shell can withstand being jumped upon – as William Coke proved before he bought the hat!

Distinguished history and prime position aside, neither the two branches of the family who own the business today nor the managing director Sue Simpson think that Lock can rest on its laurels. They want to move forward with new ranges and innovations. Besides traditional formal headwear like top hats or cokes, they also design a contemporary range of men's hats called Lock & Roll, worn by actors and musicians, indicating that wearing hats has become fashionable again.

Whereas the average age of the hat wearer ten years ago was around 50, now a lot of people in their thirties wear hats regularly. If you prefer caps, they also stock an extensive selection of handmade English caps up to size 65. Lock started doing ladies' hats around 20 years ago. These range from couture hats that are made to order and take four to six weeks to »hat-a-porter«, a collection that is ready to wear. Of course the milliners are busiest in the weeks running up to Ascot. But don't go here if you're after some crazy headgear: »We don't do crazy hats, we only do elegant hats.« states Ruth Ravenscroft, the head of the millinery team. Accordingly, even Miss Piggy once visited the shop and came away with an elegant green trilby!

Address 6 St James's Street, SW1A 1EF, Tel. +44(0)2079308874, www.lockhatters.co.uk, sales@lockhatters.co.uk | Public Transport Jubilee Piccadilly, Victoria Line, Stop Green Park | Opening Hours Mon–Fri 9am–5.30pm, Sat 9.30am–5pm | Tip Have you visited the Royals yet? Walk to Clarence House (Little St James's Street) where Prince Charles lives or Buckingham Palace from here.

60__London Taxidermy
From mice to elephants

Zebra, baboon, donkey, kiwi, koala and ladybird – these and many other species of animals populate the light and airy showroom in Wimbledon that is London Taxidermy. Owner Alexis Turner sells and hires out stuffed animals. He was always interested in natural history and had stuffed animals in his bedroom as a child.

When he started his business over 20 years ago, taxidermy was very much out of fashion – but this has changed over the last ten years. Alexis has written a book about taxidermy, which he says couldn't have been published before this revival, but now stuffed animals are literally everywhere. Alexis hires animals out for photo shoots or window displays in shops like Harrods or Hackett, and there is hardly any recent film or TV series, from Harry Potter and Sherlock Holmes to Coronation Street, that does not include an animal from London Taxidermy. Private individuals also buy them as presents or as decorations: zebras seem to go well with any interior!

Alexis either purchases antique specimens or commissions a taxidermist with what he requires. All contemporary specimens are ethically and legally sourced; no animals are killed for them, they have died as road kill or of natural causes. One of the oldest pieces he has in his showroom is a group of card-playing squirrels from 1850, similar to Walter Potter's anthropomorphic dioramas of animals mimicking human life. Taxidermy had its heyday in Victorian times. Around 1850, preservation methods were developed and specimens started to become more convincing and lifelike.

Independent schools often have collections they want to sell and for Alexis the most exciting part of his job is to discover »new« antique collections; like that of the big game hunter who lived with all his stuffed animals in a council estate in Croydon. Alexis is not a taxidermist himself but sometimes finds dead, dried-up ladybirds under his radiator. He keeps them and hires them out to clients!

Address Unit 38, Wimbledon Stadium Business Centre, Riverside Road, SW17 0BA, Tel. +44(0)7770880960, www.londontaxidermy.com, info@londontaxidermy.com | **Public Transport** District Line, Stop Southfields | **Opening Hours** Open by appointment only | **Tip** If you're a tennis fan you should visit the Wimbledon Lawn Tennis Museum (Church Road)!

61 Look Mum No Hands!

Coffee, beer and bikes

The café/bar-cum-bike workshop belongs to a new breed of bike shops that are putting the fun back into bike riding. In April 2010, the three friends Lewin Chalkley, Matthew Harper and Sam Humpheson, all enthusiastic cyclists, decided to open a place where you could have coffee, beer and something to eat while you got your bike repaired; in short, a place where they would like to hang out themselves.

Lewin and Matt had known each other for a long time, riding their choppers together in Junior School. Through their mutual love of cycling they met Sam, who had some experience of working in a bike shop. Lewin managed cafés and Matt Harper worked in finance. Everything came together when Matt was made redundant. They found an amazing location, put a coffee machine on the counter, put paint on the walls, set up a big projector screen and showed the Tour de France. Voilà! In reality it was a bit more complicated than that, but nevertheless people started coming and they were »bloody relieved«.

They put quite a lot of thought into making their business different to the usual bicycle repair shops with their grumpy mechanics. Sam heads the workshop, Lewin manages the café and Matt takes care of the business's financial side. Their approach obviously works and they have just opened a second café in Hackney. People have lots of reasons to come here: they can have breakfast while their bike is being fixed – a puncture takes about 15–20 minutes to repair – or leave their bike, go to work, come back in the evening, have a beer and relax. The bicycle-related products they sell, like mugs, t-shirts, jerseys and pants, have also become very popular. Beer is the other thing they are passionate about. They've many different kinds and try to promote small breweries. This is also the only place in London where you can have a beer and watch a cycle race. Coffee, beer and bikes: what more does a cyclist need to be happy?

Address 49 Old Street, EC1V 9HX, Tel. +44(0)2072531025, www.lookmumnohands.com, info@lookmumnohands.com | Public Transport Circle, Hammersmith, Metropolitan Line, Stop Barbican | Opening Hours Mon–Fri 7.30am–11pm, Sat 9am–11pm, Sun 9.30am–10pm | Tip Go and see Saint Bartholomew the Great (West Smithfield), one of the oldest churches in London.

62 Loop
The new yoga for men

The old sofa with its knitted and crocheted throws on the first floor
of the shop invites you to sit, select one of the beautiful yarns sur-
rounding you and start knitting or crocheting. If you don't know
what to knit, use one of the shop's own intricate patterns: probably a
Fair Isle cardigan if you are an experienced knitter, or a bobbly baby
hat if you are a beginner. You don't know how to knit? Then take one
of the classes offered here, which range from beginners to advanced
lace knitting or masterclasses with experienced knitwear designers.
Beautiful examples of knitted art and craft, like Sophie Digard's crocheted flower necklaces or scarves, are distributed all over the shop.

Susan Cropper, Loop's owner, is an art director and stylist by
trade and has always been an avid knitter. She went to art college
graduate shows and design fairs where she saw beautiful knitted
and crocheted textiles, but couldn't find where to buy the yarns to
make them. She decided to provide this place herself and founded
Loop in 2005. Five years later she moved the shop to its current location right opposite the vintage market in Camden Passage. Here
she stocks yarns from all over the world, most of them made from
natural fibres and often hand-dyed. They range from organic cotton
or linen, hand-dyed baby camel and silk to chunky Peruvian High-
land wool.

The shop sells single knitting and crochet patterns as well as a
big selection of books. A lot of the classes taught here fill up very
quickly. Susan describes the resurgence of crafts as a reaction to the
unification of the high street. People want a few things that are bespoke to them. As an afterthought she adds: »Women of the previous generation wanted to distance themselves from domestic crafts.
Today independent women have less to prove and can go back to
craft.« Knitting and other crafts are more popular than ever, and not
only women take them up: in the media, knitting is being hailed as
the »new yoga« for men!

Address 15 Camden Passage, N1 8EA, Tel. +44(0)2072881160, www.loopknitting.com, loopknittingshop@yahoo.co.uk | Public Transport Northern Line, Stop Angel | Opening Hours Tues, Weds, Fri, Sat 11am–6pm, Thurs 11am –7.30pm, Sun 12 pm–5pm | Tip Visit Islington's farmers market on a Sunday (Chapel Market, Penton Street). Here you'll find fresh seasonal food and flowers.

63_Luna & Curious
Beasties and other banquets

Calvert Avenue has an understated charm that attracts trendy stores and businesses. This is exactly the right setting for Luna & Curious, an enchanting white shop that sells beautifully crafted objects and clothing. The lamps here, made from white umbrellas, diffuse the light and set the background for the shop's unique products – although, adding a bit of bite, customers are greeted by a rather menacing-looking fox!

The store was founded in 2006 by a group of seven designers. Over the years the design collective has changed and the shop moved from Brick Lane to its current location three years ago. Today Polly George, Rheanna Lingham and Kaoru Parry own the business jointly as a design consortium. Rheanna makes bold and beautiful costume jewellery from feathers, metal and porcelain and Polly and Kaoru are ceramicists. Polly's predominantly white all-English bone china is produced for her in Stoke-on-Trent. She designs delicate teapots, cups and mugs populated by butterflies, and miniature porcelain busts, so-called cress heads, which are sold with cotton wool and cress seeds to get their »hair« growing. Her ceramics are complemented by Kaoru's inventive but more colourful approach, such as the Basilica Mugs in black and white inspired by 17th-century Venetian church tiles.

Besides their own collections, Rheanna, Kaoru and Polly also sell items by carefully selected designers from all over the world. They stock unusual stockings and tights from Les Queues de Sardines in France, children's clothing from Denmark and miniature architectural model kits made from metal in England. They also help young designers to start their career. The rule is that at least two of them have to agree before they showcase someone's work in the shop.

Their debut collection as a design consortium is the Beastie Banquet Range with a bull's head cheese cover, salt and pepper pig trotters, and a large tankard: a welcome addition to a medieval or indeed any other banquet!

The Beastie Banquet

Designed by Luna & Curious
Hand made by artisans in Stoke On Trent, England

English Oak Chopping Board £50
Pigs Trotter Salt and Pepper £45

Address 24–26 Calvert Avenue, E2 7JP, Tel. +44(0)2032220034, www.lunaandcurious.com, info@lunaandcurious.com | Public Transport Northern Line, Stop Old Street | Opening Hours Mon–Sat 11am–6pm, Sun 11am–5pm | Tip Calvert Avenue leads to Arnold Circus, home to one of the oldest social housing estates in London. A pretty bandstand was erected in the middle of the square as part of the development.

64__Made.com
Design that doesn't cost the world

The Made.com showroom is an open secret tucked away on the ninth floor of Newcombe House, Notting Hill Gate. From here you can enjoy wonderful views across the whole of London while sipping a cup of coffee and relaxing on your favourite sofa or armchair.

For any fan of designer furniture, Made.com is definitely a must. They collaborate with established designers such as Allegra Hicks and Casa Estudio, award prizes to new designers and produce their furniture. One example is the »Lovebird Sofa«, the result of a competition organised in collaboration with the Design Museum to find the most innovative 2-seater sofa. Je-Uk Kim's prize-winning model was inspired by two lovebirds and is a multifunctional sofa with two pull-out units: a coffee-table-cum-storage and a large cushion that turns the sofa into an ottoman. The furniture you can see in the showroom ranges from very contemporary pieces like Hugh Leader-Williams's set of dining table and stools (all foldable for easy storage) made from spun steel and solid ash to classics like the »Flynn collection«, sofas and armchairs inspired by Chesterfields but with cleaner lines and a more modern feel. The good news is that all these pieces are available at very affordable prices, often much cheaper than furniture you can buy in the average high street store.

So what is the secret behind these consumer friendly prices? The founders of the business, Ning Li, Brent Hoberman, Chloe Macintosh and Julien Callède, came up with a unique concept. Usually high-end designer furniture passes through several middlemen, resulting in high prices for the consumer. So Made.com simply cut out the middleman! There is no warehouse or physical store. The furniture is sold online and all the orders for one piece are grouped every week and are made to order directly by the producers. Amazingly, this proximity to designers and makers allows Made.com's beautiful pieces to be up to 70% cheaper than an ordinary furniture shop.

Address Ninth Floor, Newcombe House, 45 Notting Hill Gate, W11 3LQ. Tel.
+44(0)8455576888, www.made.com, ninthfloor@made.com | **Public Transport** Central,
District Line, Stop Notting Hill Gate | **Opening Hours** Mon–Fri 11.30am–7.30pm,
Sat–Sun 10.30am–6pm | **Tip** Visit the Museum of Brands, Packaging and Advertising
(2 Colville Mews).

65 Maggs Bros.
Napoleon's penis or his signature?

Maggs Bros. resides in 50 Berkeley Square, known in the 1900s as the most haunted house in London. It was said that the spirit of a young woman who had committed suicide there haunted the attic. In Victorian times several deaths occurred in the house, but since Maggs Bros. moved here in 1936 no other phenomena have been reported.

Uriah Maggs founded the business in 1853 and now it is one of the oldest antiquarian book dealers in the world, still run by the family and currently managed by Edward Maggs. Over the course of its long history, Maggs Bros. has managed to make some fantastic deals, among them purchases of Napoleon's penis, two Gutenberg Bibles, the Codex Sinaiticus and a copy of the first book printed in England, William Caxton's »The Canterbury Tales«.

Today the antiquarian sells and buys books from all over the world. Different experts occupy different floors of the large house. One of them is Titus Boeder, who has worked here for 18 years and deals with Japanese and Chinese books, photographs and maps. He read Chinese with Japanese at university and lived in China and Japan. He specialises in Japanese photo books as well as items relating to post-War Japanese graphic design. There are also other departments such as Travel, Continental, Illuminations or Counterculture. The Autograph and Manuscript department run by Polly Beauwin is particularly fascinating. Here you can find documents signed by Oliver Cromwell, Marlborough, Wellington or Nelson, letters from the surgeon who looked after the Elephant man, or a receipt for spying from 1386. Autographs are collected by libraries or museums, but if you want to start your own collection you can find interesting items for surprisingly little money. Start with a letter from Blücher written just before Waterloo, and then move on to Napoleon, who dictated his letters to a secretary and only added his signature at the end because his handwriting was so awful. So which would you prefer, his penis or his signature?

Address 50 Berkeley Square, W1J 5BA, Tel. +44(0)2074937160, www.maggs.com, enquiries@maggs.com | **Public Transport** Jubilee, Piccadilly, Victoria Line, Stop Green Park | **Opening Hours** Mon–Fri 9.30am–5pm | **Tip** You could have lunch on one of the many benches in Berkeley Square. Afterwards, Rolls-Royce fans can take a peek through the window of Rolls-Royce Motor Cars London (15 Berkeley Square).

66 __ The Map House
The island of California

The Map House is located in fashionable Beauchamp Place in Knightsbridge and the shop is as distinguished as the area it resides in. Alfred Sifton and Francis Praed founded it in 1907 as a map selling and publishing business. They have supplied maps to Ernest Shackleton and Winston Churchill and supplied the Royal Family until the 1950s.

Subsequently they specialised and are now the biggest sellers of fine antique maps in the world. Around 20,000 of the maps they hold are listed but they have many more that are not. The oldest map they stock is the world map from Hartman Schedel's Nuremberg Chronicle published in 1493. Printed when Columbus had just returned from his first voyage, Schedel's map still depicts the Ptolemaic world view, not taking into account Columbus's discovery that was to change the perception of our planet.

So what are maps actually for? Nowadays we assume that a map helps you find your way from A to B. However, Philip Curtis, director at The Map House, knows better and explains that this function of maps has evolved only recently. »Not that long ago people didn't need maps because they never ventured more than 20 miles from the place they were born. Maps showed an idea of the world. They were representations of power and influence.« A Chinese map from 1810 demonstrates this beautifully. Made for the Qing emperor's court it was the most precise map of China to date, but the further you get from China the less accurate it gets. Britain became a very small dot compared to Holland, depicted as a slightly larger island.

Besides maps they also sell globes, one of them the largest globe ever made commercially in 1880, of which The Map House holds one of two known examples. The other is displayed in the Natural History Museum in Vienna. You can definitely buy beautiful maps here, but don't try and use them to go to the island of California!

Address 54 Beauchamp Place, SW3 1NY, Tel. +44(0)2075894325, www.themaphouse.com, maps@themaphouse.com | **Public Transport** Piccadilly Line, Stop Knightsbridge | **Opening Hours** Mon–Fri 10am–6pm, Sat 10.30am–5pm | **Tip** It's your choice: tackle one of the major museums here or go to Harrods!

67 Marchpane
Through the looking glass

In the shop window ivy winds around illustrated editions of »Alice in Wonderland«, and above the entrance a blue star shows the way. Inside Marchpane – the name itself reminiscent of old-fashioned delicacies – two life-sized daleks from the legendary British science fiction TV series »Doctor Who« greet visitors.

Kenneth Fuller has sold illustrated antiquarian children's books in this fantastic environment since 1989. He specialises in »Alice in Wonderland« books: first editions, illustrated editions, Alice in German, Russian, Chinese and Japanese – the book has been translated into at least 97 languages. Customers from all over the world come here to find special editions of »Alice in Wonderland«, »Winnie the Pooh« or »Peter Pan«. These books are given to children and grandchildren on their birthdays and other special occasions and often will become treasured possessions passed on to the following generations. »But Alice is more than a popular children's book,« explains Kenneth Fuller, »the mad hatter's tea party for example was used in satires and caricatures of the time as a metaphor for political and social problems. It influenced the following generations, authors from James Joyce to Douglas Adams, and became part of our cultural heritage.« Kenneth is very interested in the cultural and historical background of children's books.

Another of his collections are so-called »chapbooks«, small illustrated books aimed at the 18th- and 19th-century working classes that reflect historical and political events. He also stocks a number of first editions of authors like Enid Blyton and Elinor M. Brent-Dyer published during the Second World War. A particularly fascinating example of World War II books are the small illustrated brochures trying to explain the harsh reality of war and bombardments to children. Children's books are not just children's books to Kenneth. Every one of them reveals a whole new world!

Address 16 Cecil Court, Charing Cross Road, WC2N 4HE, Tel. +44(0)207836 8661, www.marchpane.com Public Transport Northern, Piccadilly Line, Stop Leicester Square Opening Hours Mon–Sat 10.30am–6pm Around Leicester Square you will find the largest cinemas in Britain. If you're lucky you might spot one or two famous actors arriving for a film premiere!

68 Michael German Antiques

Walking with canes

Arms and armour, walking canes or maritime and whaling works of art; which is your collecting field? Even if you don't collect any of these things at present, you will probably change your mind after seeing all the interesting and unusual pieces in Michael German Antiques: beautiful crafted objects made by whalers when they were at sea; antique guns, swords and medieval armour; and finally walking canes, from a cane carried by Ralph Fiennes as Charles Dickens to a braying donkey cane.

The shop's founder Michael German has been in the antiques trade for a long time. He had several businesses and finally moved to Kensington Church Street in 1982. The shop is a collector's Mecca that rarely advertises but will be found nevertheless by the discerning collector. Today it is run by Michael's son-in-law, Dominic Strickland, who also knows of the joys and perils of collecting. »For me the best part is if you find something wonderful, show it to a collector and he gets as excited as you are.«

Dominic was an architect and took a course at Christie's before entering the world of collectors. He explains that arms and armour is an established collecting field, whereas collecting canes is rather more recent. Michael German has been a pioneer in this area, attending walking cane exhibitions and organising conferences.

In the shop you will find canes from around 1860 to 1910. In the Victorian era canes were not used to aid walking; they were a dress accessory for ladies and gentlemen alike. You weren't properly dressed if you didn't carry a walking cane. For every new outfit you had to have a matching cane: an evening model refined with jewels or gold, an everyday one, and at the weekend a cane with a folk-art handle. A pity that we no longer walk with such elegant canes today – but at least you can collect them!

Address 38b Kensington Church Street, W8 4BX, Tel. +44(0)2079372771,
www.antiquecanes.com, info@antiquecanes.com | Public Transport Circle, District Line,
Stop High Street Kensington | Opening Hours Mon–Fri 10am–5pm, Sat 10am–1pm |
Tip Kensington Palace Orangery (Kensington Gardens) serves afternoon tea in style!

69___M. Manze

What's in the pie?

It's impossible to talk about traditional food in London without mentioning pie and mash! Pie and mash is a working-class food invented in South East London in the 19th century. Workers' food had to be cheap and easy to prepare. Pies were the ideal »fast food« as they were transportable and protected by their crust. They were either filled with eel or with minced meat. Although traditional pie and mash shops are getting increasingly rare today, there are still some around.

The oldest of them is M. Manze, whose Tower Bridge shop was first opened in 1892 and has remained pretty much unchanged ever since. It was originally founded and run by Robert Cooke until his son-in-law Michele Manze took over in 1902. Michele came from a small village in Southern Italy. His family started an ice-cream business next door to the pie shop, which it ran until Michele felt that something more substantial was needed and branched out into the pie, mash and eel trade. In the years that followed, his family opened several shops and three of them are still in business today, run by the Manze family.

So what do you actually get if you order pie and mash and eels? The pies are freshly baked in the shop on the day. The pastry is handmade, rolled out and filled with beef that is minced immediately before use. The potatoes for the mash are peeled and cooked on site. The eels, either jellied or stewed, are cooked in the shop and the »liquor«…is not alcoholic but a green parsley sauce with a secret ingredient, served with the eel.

The legendary shop was and is frequented by many celebrities. Who knows, you might encounter David Beckham, who is said to eat here when he's in England – or his wife Victoria, who has given an interview in the shop. Now that you know what's in your pie and mash, you can either have it delivered or eat it on site, enjoying the beautifully tiled historic interior of the shop and the company of the lovely Manze Ladies, renowned for their friendly service.

MANZE
tea towel

TO OUR EEL CUSTOMERS

WE REGRET TO INFORM YOU THAT EEL STOCKS
ARE EXTREMELY LOW, AS A CONSEQUENCE
PRICES ARE CONTINUALLY INCREASING.

IT IS POSSIBLE STOCKS OF EELS MAY
DISAPPEAR COMPLETELY IN THE NEAR FUTURE.

M.MANZE

M. MANZE   M. MANZE

TOWER BRIDGE ROAD   PECKHAM HIGH STRE

EEL & PIE HOUSE

M.MANZE

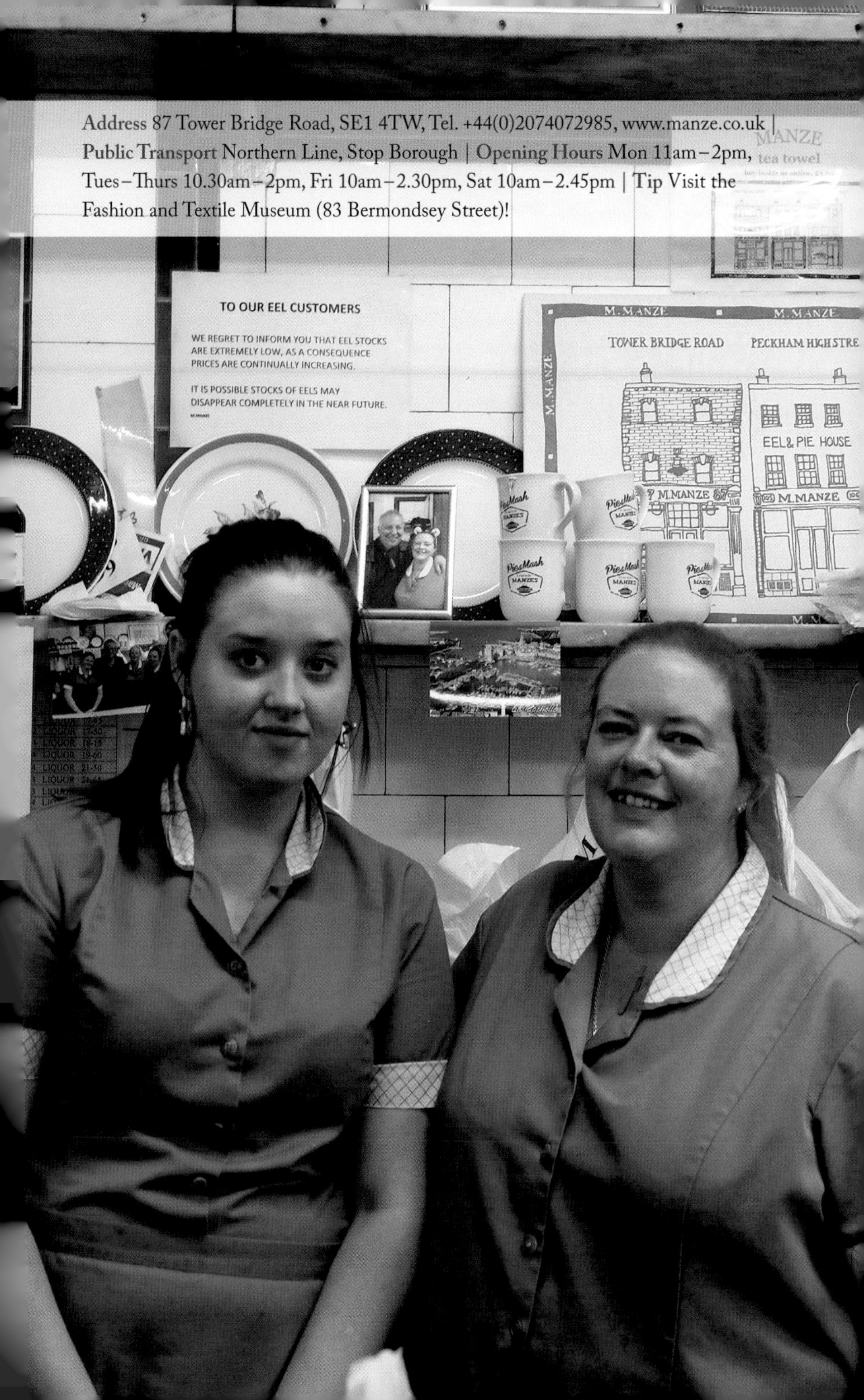

70 _ The Moomin Shop
Furry philosophers

Most of us were children when we read the Moomin books or comics or saw the animations, and thus a visit to the Moomin Shop can be like a reunion with old friends that you haven't seen for ages. »This is how many visitors react,« says Patrick, the owner of the Moomin shop. »People from all over the world, even rugby players, come to the shop and can't stop smiling when they see their favourite characters again.«

He reacquainted himself with the hippopotamus-like trolls when he organised an exhibition for their 55th birthday in Edinburgh. The Moomins had played an important role in his childhood and he was excited that they were coming back into his life. At the exhibition he met Sophia, the niece and executor of Tove Jansson, the Finnish-Swedish author and illustrator of the Moomins. The exhibition was so successful that Patrick was inspired to open a shop in London selling Moomin books in different editions and languages, t-shirts, mugs, soft toys and other Moomin products from all over the world.

Why are these funny creatures so fascinating? Is it their philosophical nature or the beautifully drawn characters? Although they are children's stories, Tove Jansson never tried to hide reality or even death in her tales. The books are often about how people are different but need each other nevertheless. Patrick's favourite character is Moomintroll, the stories' gentle and maybe somewhat naïve main character. Others prefer the Snork, Snork Maiden or Little My. For example, Moomintroll's friend, the lonely traveller Snufkin, is especially popular in Japan, whereas English men for no discernable reason find the Groke irresistible – a cold growling creature everyone is afraid of because it can freeze the ground under its feet.

The Moomins live all together in idyllic Moominvalley, somewhere in Finland. Who can resist these furry philosophers?

Address 43 Covent Garden Market, WC2E 8RF, Tel. +44(0)2072407057,
www.themoominshop.com | Public Transport Piccadilly Line, Stop Covent Garden |
Opening Hours Mon–Sat 10am–8pm, Sun 11am–5pm | Tip Take some time to watch
the many performance artists in and around Covent Garden!

71___Mysteries
Vibrating stones

Lava lamps, incense, crystals, dream catchers, worry dolls, astro-cards, angels and buddhas, plus an eclectic bunch of customers ranging from Nicole Kidman and Anne Hathaway to the homeless – is this an adequate description of Mysteries, the esoteric shop in Monmouth Street? For Branca Geffin, the shop is much more. She sees it as a centre for body, spirit and soul.

Besides esoteric products, courses in hand reading, tarot and spiritual development are offered here. You can also book sessions with clairvoyants and psychic or aura readers on the Mysteries website. When Branca's husband opened the business many years ago, Mysteries was the first shop of its kind in Europe. Nobody believed that you could earn money with something that was so »mysterious«. Today, 31 years later, Branca manages the shop following her husband's retirement three years ago because of health issues. He still develops ideas for the business in the background but is no longer actively involved. Over the last few years the products they stock have changed. They offer fewer books and more healing crystals from amethyst to tourmaline, which sell really well. They now have the biggest collection of healing stones in London.

So why do crystals heal? »Minerals vibrate to certain resonances,« says Branca. »Our body can get out of sync because of stress, environment or pollution and crystals realign areas of your body.«

It is important to Branca that customers come to the shop, take their time, touch the stones and find the one that is right for them. You can't download a mineral from the internet! In our society, where immediate gratification is imperative, this can be a challenge. For Branca, Mysteries has a special atmosphere. She strongly believes that the shop is a catalyst that makes people change their lives. Once the door of the shop was left open for a whole night. Nothing happened.

Address 9–11 Monmouth Street, WC2H 9DA, Tel. +44(0)2072403688, www.mysteries.co.uk, shop@mysteries.co.uk | Public Transport Piccadilly Line, Stop Covent Garden | Opening Hours Mon 10.02am–18.55pm, Tues 9.54am–19.07pm, Weds 9.59am–18.58pm, Thurs 10am–7.01pm, Fri 9.57am–7.15pm, Sat 9.56am–6.50pm, Sun 13pm–6pm | Tip Go to Neal's Yard, a small alleyway where you can have a coffee, buy natural cosmetics and British cheese.

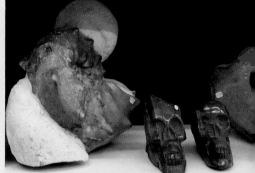

72 Mystical Fairies
Which fairy?

Where can you still experience real magic? Easy: the fairy shop in Hampstead! Even small girls who never stop talking are dumbstruck when they enter the shop's pink fairy wonderland. Everywhere you look glitters in pink, silver and gold. Flower fairies, woodland fairies and meadow fairies, Tinker Bell from Peter Pan, fairy children, grandmother fairies – and not to forget the tooth fairy, who brings children presents or money for lost teeth – all inhabit this magical shop, which is tucked away in a small pedestrian street in Hampstead.

Anything a fairy or a princess needs you will find here: from fairy nighties, princess costumes, fairy lip gloss and fairy dust to fairy jewellery boxes and small magic doors to attach to the skirting board through which the little people can enter a child's room at night. A little bit of fairy psychology: most little girls will identify with a fairy who has the same hair colour as they have. Although the magic here has its biggest effect on little girls, little boys can also turn into kings, pirates, magicians or knights. Once in the shop, you will have a problem in getting your children out of it.

When Veronica Ford founded the shop in 2002 her own daughter was at the »fairy-tale age«. She found it difficult to find shops that welcomed small children. As she loved all things pink and sparkly herself, she decided to open a place where children were not only welcome, but could live out their fantasies and love of fairies and princesses. Veronica uses the knowledge she has gained about these enchanted creatures over the years to organise elaborately themed parties and workshops where little fairies and princesses learn how to use fairy dust, put on fairy lipstick or do princess craft. Veronica also works with several charities that support children in need. Only one question remains: which fairy would your daughter choose?

Address 12 Flask Walk, NW3 1HE, Tel. +44(0)2074311888, www.mysticalfairies.co.uk, sales@mysticalfairies.co.uk | Public Transport Northern Line, Stop Hampstead | Opening Hours Mon–Sat 10am–6pm, Sun 11am–6pm | Tip Opposite the fairy shop, Judy Green's Garden Store (11 Flask Walk) has a lot of beautiful things for older princesses!

73__N1 Garden Centre

Heavenly bamboo

Walking down a residential road between Islington and Hackney, you suddenly come across rows of brightly coloured bedding plants. This is N1 Garden Centre, occupying the space of an old stableyard and button factory.

Entering, you will see perennials, bedding plants, houseplants and shrubs, all beautifully displayed in the small space. Creative director Paul Holt is responsible for the inspirational displays, combining colour, shape height and texture with amazing results. In the different sections you will find a good selection of the usual plants you would grow in a town garden but there is also always something less common – a display, a shrub or a perennial you've never seen before.

Joel Beckman, the managing director, explains that they follow three principles: »good plants, good advice and great experience«. Good plants means that they source plants from small independent nurseries in the south of England (the outdoor plants even come with a two-year guarantee). Good advice: they hire staff with either a horticultural background or a good knowledge of plants and gardening. The staff should also be able to »demystify« gardening for young or inexperienced gardeners – after all, it should be fun, not a chore! Most of the customers are locals and from 2014 onwards, they are also offering a garden maintenance service.

The initiator of all this is Beryl Henderson, who opened N1 Garden Centre because she felt a place to buy good quality plants was missing in the North London area where she lived. In 1998 she took the plunge and the business became so successful that they went on to open the W6 Garden Centre in West London only a few years later. Joel, who has a finance background but also went to horticultural college, manages both centres. His favourite plant – among others – is Heavenly Bamboo Nandina, sporting lovely coloured foliage and red berries.

Address The Old Button Factory, 25a Englefield Road, N1 4EU, Tel. +44(020)79233553, www.n1gardencentre.co.uk, info@n1gc.co.uk | Public Transport London Overground towards Stratford, Stop Dalston Kingsland | Opening Hours Mon–Sun 9.30am–5pm | Tip If you are in the area on the first Sunday in February, go to the annual clowns' international service in Holy Trinity Church, Dalston (Beechwood Road), attended by clowns in full costume and followed by a public performance!

74__New Century Barbers Shop

An ancient trade

The barbershop on one of the corners of Fortis Green Road in Muswell Hill is a local institution. The outside, with its revolving white and red barber pole – a reminder of the times when barbers still let blood and hung out their bloodied bandages – could feature in any mid-20th-century ad. Upon entering, broad-leaved climbing plants, yellow and black 1950s interiors and retro signs – »Clean hair is healthy hair. Have a shampoo« – will make you feel like you have travelled back in time. Owner John Nicola has been here since 1989, but the shop has existed as a barbershop since 1906. Today five people work here full time, offering haircuts, shaves and beard trims. Any of these will take ten to thirty minutes. But you have to be a man to get your hair done here, because this is an old-school gent's barbershop!

Like everything else, gent's haircuts follow changing fashions and John will do whatever customers ask for – although if it gets too weird he will tell them: »Don't tell anybody you had a haircut here, because to me it doesn't look like a haircut!« A lot of the customers are local and come on a regular basis. John has known some of them for many years; he first met them as children and now they are married and bring their own children. It sometimes happens that he gets to groom four generations of one family!

There's no typical customer: doctors, footballers, judges or snooker players, famous actors or musicians all come. But whoever it is sitting in the black chairs, they all tell him stories. They talk about football or give John racing tips, they mention their marriages and divorces, they tell him about their health, their families and where they are going on holiday. Many people are lonely and have nobody to talk to, and he likes to listen. This hasn't changed for centuries: the barber's is an ancient trade.

Address 119 Fortis Green Road, N10 3HP, Tel. +44(0)2088835092 | **Public Transport**
Northern Line, Stop East Finchley, then bus 102 to Muswell Hill Road | **Opening Hours**
Mon–Sat 8am–7pm | **Tip** Go for a stroll and discover Muswell Hill's nearly entirely
Edwardian architecture.

75_ The Old Curiosity Shop
Dickens and designer shoes

The Old Curiosity Shop is one of London's hidden gems. You either stumble across it by chance or know of it beforehand. Tucked away in Portsmouth Street, behind Shaftesbury Avenue, a visitor wouldn't usually come across it as it is located between the buildings of the London School of Economics, away from the main shopping areas. It is thought to be the model for Charles Dickens's »old curiosity shop« in his novel of the same name. At the beginning of the book, Little Nell and her grandfather live here and sell odds and ends.

When Dickens published his novel in 1841, the shop probably already looked out of place with its compact build and Tudor beams. Dickens also created its name, because it only started to be called »The Old Curiosity Shop« after he gave it an important role in his novel. The house was built in 1567 using timber from old ships and survived the Great Fire of 1666 as well as the bombs of the Second World War undamaged.

With its low ceilings, dark wooden floors and slanted light falling through the windows, today the shop provides an enchanted setting for the shoes of Japanese footwear designer Daita Kimura, who opened his shop here in 1992. He designs shoes that are as unusual as the building they are sold in. At first glance his shoes often look simple, like his black patent leather sandals, but their special features are revealed in their detail: they can be folded and stored flat in a suitcase.

There are also shoes for smelly feet with a removable stopper at the front. His signature shoes are »Hog-toes«, looking as if someone has cut off their tip and sown on a flat piece of leather instead. Despite these unusual details, all his shoes are extremely wearable, well made and simply beautiful. If you ask Daita what motivated him to open his shop in this building he answers: »It was available and I just rented it.« Dickens and designer shoes: well, they do say that opposites attract …

Address 13–14 Portsmouth Street, WC2A 2ES, Tel. +44(0)74059891, info@curiosityuk.com | **Public Transport** Central, Piccadilly Line, Stop Holborn | **Opening Hours** Mon–Sat 10.30am–7pm | **Tip** The Hunterian Museum (35–43 Lincoln's Inn Fields) contains one of the oldest collections of zoological, pathological and anatomical specimens in Britain, based on the collection of the surgeon John Hunter (1728–1793).

76_Ooh-la-la!

On the road to Scotland

Holloway Road is one of the main shopping streets in North London. A lot of traffic passes through it as it carries the A1. Along this major thoroughfare there are railway stations, universities and major stores – and Oh-la-la! Julian, one of the sellers in the shop, claims that »Holloway Road is the true London, which still hasn't been touched by massive commerce.« He works together with David, the shop's proprietor, who introduces himself as »one of the people who sells the mad vintage funky antiques.«

Since he bought it in 1996, the shop has gone through phases of vintage, retro and house clearing and a phase during which it sold mainly sofas. Today it's an eclectic mix, mainly owing to the fact that it is hired out to different people who sell antiques from their areas of expertise: specialists for lights, clothes or furniture.

David greatly enjoys that the shop is full of surprises and you never know what you will find when you come inside: maybe a Victorian doll's house, a 1920s dress or a horse from a merry-go-round! David and Julian both have professional backgrounds. David worked for Phillips, which later became Bonham, and does furniture and furniture restoration; Julian specialises in musical instruments. He used to work for Christie's, where he revealed that a guitar allegedly owned by Elvis Presley was a fake. As they have been here for such a long time a lot of the things they sell are brought into the shop. They're known to locals, but many media or film people also come here to rent furniture or other items – parts of the film »Notes on a Scandal« were filmed here. David admits that he doesn't earn much with the shop but it suits his temperament: »It's like an artist not wanting to charge too much for his art.« At the moment Julian is teaching him how to play the guitar. Oh, and did you know that Holloway Road is part of the old Roman road that goes from the Thames all the way to Scotland?

Address 147 Holloway Road, N7 8LX, Tel. +44(0)2076090455 | **Public Transport** Victoria Line, Stop Highbury, Islington | **Opening Hours** Mon–Sat 10am–6pm | **Tip** Fans of Italian Futurism shouldn't miss the Estorick Collection of modern Italian art (39a Canonbury Square).

77 — Opera Opera
Framed

The distinctive metal and glass front with a door handle shaped like a pair of glasses makes this shop in Covent Garden's Long Acre stand out. Opera Opera is probably the only optician's in the world with its own factory producing custom-made frames. The family business has existed since 1978; the factory opened in 1988.

In contrast to the current trend of ordering ready-made glasses on the internet, here the individual customer and his or her requirements take centre stage. A qualified optometrist examines your eyes, taking various measurements. Then comes the hard part: you have to choose. Would you like Johnny Depp, John Lennon or Buddy Holly frames? Or maybe the glasses Dustin Hoffmann wore in »Tootsie«? Opera Opera mainly produces frames from block acetate, a material that can be molded into different shapes and is available in many colours. They also sell carefully chosen frames made by other small companies as well as vintage models. Many of the shop's own frames have become classics over the years.

Can you design your own made-to-measure glasses? »Of course,« says Greg, who will also patiently help you to choose from the models in the shop, »although it's a bit more expensive.« Like everyone who works here, he is very passionate about frames. Discreetly he explains that many celebrities order custom-made glasses but would prefer to remain anonymous. There are also collectors who own more than 20 different pairs. One of their most unusual commissions was a pair of glasses for a figure at Madame Tussaud's.

Back to choosing a frame: a monocle is out of the question, even though they are very fashionable at the moment according to Greg. A chicken, a fish, a butterfly or a dolphin frame? Anything you could possibly imagine can be made. Or the classical model Greg recommends? Whatever model you choose, you can be sure that Opera Opera will find a frame that suits you!

Address 98 Long Acre, Covent Garden, WC2E 9NR, Tel. +44(0)2078369246, www.operaopera.net | Public Transport Piccadilly Line, Stop Covent Garden | Opening Hours Mon−Sat 10am−6pm | Tip Book tickets for a performance at the nearby Royal Opera House (Bow Street)!

78 Past Caring
Back to the 70s

Do you like furniture and carpets with orange and brown geometric patterns? Pictures of scantily clad gypsy ladies? Brown and yellow glazed rustic pottery? Floppy hats, disco-fashion? Blue and red glassware? In short, if you're a fan of the 70s you'll find everything you need to furnish your house – or dress yourself – here. Past Caring stocks old things from the 1950s to the 1970s. The shop on 54 Essex Road was aptly established in 1973 by Mr. and Mrs. Osborne, and a few years ago their son Carl took over. It started out as a clothes shop and later changed to include bric-a-brac, china and furniture. Now, imagine you are either an avid vintage collector or a set designer for a 1970s TV series.

The outside is promising: lots of old chairs, mirrors and a mannequin from the period. Entering the premises your gaze is drawn to bright blood-red ceramics from West Germany, which have become quite fashionable again and will add a splash of colour to any interior. Venture further inside the shop and you will find many more items to furnish your 1970s flat. For the living room, you can have Spanish flamenco dolls – or would you prefer Japanese geishas? And you definitely need an old dial telephone! For the kitchen, a light blue mincer would be nice; and don't miss out the tea service decorated with brown sunflowers!

You should also get a 1970s suitcase in which to take all your purchases away. Now proceed to the back of the shop, where you will find a matching outfit complete with tie, hat and flower-print blazer. If you would rather make your own clothes, you can also buy sewing patterns of the time here. The 1970s aficionado will definitely find the best pieces downstairs in the basement. Teak sideboards, cabinets, tables, lamps, sofas and chairs, as well as old typewriters or oil paintings featuring galloping horses will complete your authentic 1970s interior. All done: you've successfully time travelled back to the 70s!

Address 54 Essex Road, N1 8LR | Public Transport Northern Line, Stop Angel |
Opening Hours Mon–Sat 12–6pm | Tip Just around the corner (14 Dagmar Passage),
you'll find the well-known Little Angel Theatre, which is a puppet theatre. They put on
great shows, especially at Christmas!

79 __ Paxton and Whitfield

A smell that wakes the dead

»We've always been here and we've always sold cheese.« This could well be the motto of Paxton and Whitfield in Jermyn Street, because it's very close to the truth: for 150 years, the cheese shop with its beautiful black and gold frontage has resided here among all the gentlemen's outfitters.

The origins of the shop go even further back to the 18th century, when Sam Cullum set up a cheese stall in Aldwych in 1742. He later acquired two partners, Mr. Paxton and Mr. Whitfield, and the shop moved to Jermyn Street to cater to wealthier customers. Over the years the shop has had several different owners, but it has always remained a cheese shop except for a brief period during World War II, when it turned into a grocery store due to the shortage in cheese.

The taste in cheeses however has evolved and changed over time. For many years, continental cheeses from France or the Netherlands were much in demand, but in the last decades the British cheese industry has experienced something of a Renaissance. While classic cheeses like Stilton and Cheddar have always been popular, now traditional and artisan cheesemaking has come very much into its own. Small businesses produce an amazing variety of artisan cheeses, ranging from Stinking Bishop – a soft cheese made famous by Wallace and Gromit in a scene where its smell revives Wallace from the dead – to Caerphilly, a white hard cheese from Wales originally developed to balance out the salt loss of the coalminers, who worked long shifts underground.

70 % of the 200 cheeses sold here are produced in the UK, and some of them are made exclusively for the shop – such as Aldwych goat's cheese from Somerset, made from the unpasteurised milk of white Saneen, Toggenburg, British Alpine and Anglo-Nubian goats. As the queues at Paxton and Whitfield are sometimes pretty long – especially before Christmas – the shop will hopefully continue to sell cheese for well over another 150 years.

Address 93 Jermyn Street, SW1Y 6JE, Tel. +44(0)2079300259, www.paxtonandwhitfield.co.uk, jermynstreet@paxtonandwhitfield.co.uk | **Public Transport** Piccadilly Line, Stop Piccadilly Circus | **Opening Hours** Mon–Sat 9.30am–6pm | **Tip** There's a small market in front of St James's Church, Piccadilly (197 Piccadilly). It sells food on Mondays, antiques on Tuesdays and crafts on Wednesdays to Saturdays.

80__Pentreath & Hall

What we love

The first things you notice upon entering the shop are the beautiful white plaster casts on the mustard yellow back wall. There is also a fireplace, a dresser with a lovely collection of crockery, and a colourful armchair that invites you to sit down, read a book or simply look at the nice things that are displayed throughout the shop.

The person responsible for the lovely displays is shop manager Robin Tabor, who is also happy to share his knowledge about the shop's history. It actually came into existence more or less by accident. Ben Pentreath, one of the shop's founders, needed more office space for his expanding architectural practice and he decided to move into the little shop on Rugby Street just across from his office. He installed an office in the back and in the front opened a little shop together with his friend Bridie Hall. Bridie is a decorative artist and maker and sells her own collection of decorative trays and objects in the store. The shop became very popular and the office eventually had to move out of the back room. In 2013, Ben and Birdie officially joined forces and »Ben Pentreath« became »Pentreath & Hall«.

The secret behind Ben and Birdie's success is that they only source and sell what they love themselves. For example, there are the lovely plaster casts made by the master plaster caster Peter Hone. These are mostly reproductions from 18th-century casts and Hone's own extraordinary flat full of casts has been featured in several books and magazines.

Pentreath & Hall also stock prints of 20th-century artists such as Eric Ravilious, beautiful trays designed by Bridie, and Leeds Pottery and Spring Resin Lamps by Marianna Kennedy. Ben also visits antique dealers and local auctions to source ornaments, old maps or single pieces of furniture. The shop is a wild mixture of everything Ben and Bridie love – which is precisely why it feels just like the perfect living room!

Address 17 Rugby Street, WC1N 3QT, Tel. +44(0)2074302526, www.pentreath-hall.com, shop@pentreath-hall.com | Public Transport Piccadilly Line, Stop Russell Square | Opening Hours Mon–Sat 11am–6pm | Tip The Charles Dickens Museum (48 Doughty Street) is the only remaining London home of the famous writer. It hosts a collection of Dickens artifacts.

81 Persephone Books
Dove-grey secrets

Lamb's Conduit Street in Bloomsbury has become known over the last few years as a hub for avant-garde men's fashion. In the midst of this masculine »cutting-edge-ness«, Persephone Books is an island of dove-grey old-fashioned femininity, a sort of antidote to men's fashion. It prints and sells forgotten or neglected (mostly) female mid-20th century authors.

The first thing you notice about the shop is that everything is grey. The shop front is grey and when you cross the threshold, you will see that all of the books are grey too. They all have the same distinctive dove-grey jacket and cream label, but when you open them, the endpapers are all different and feature beautiful colours and patterns. They match the mood and date of the book in question and are sourced from fabrics of the time. Take Constance Maud's suffragette novel »No Surrender« as an example. Gerald Duckworth, Virginia Woolf's half-brother, first published it in 1911. Its endpaper is a 1913 Omega Workshop block-print design in the suffragette colours purple, green and white.

Persephone Books now has over 100 titles in print by around 50–60 authors, which the founder Nicola Beauman chooses, consulting everyone who works here. Nicola founded the business in 1998 after inheriting some money, fulfilling her dream of promoting neglected female writers. Prior to this she already had a career as a writer of biographies. She started out with a mail-order business and the shop opened in 2001. Here, you can wander through piles of grey books and receive excellent recommendations from the friendly and knowledgeable staff. Whatever your preferences are, from poetry or ghost stories to diaries and cookery books, you'll find something of interest. No wonder that many book groups have chosen Persephone as their favourite hunting ground. Each second Thursday of the month the shop fills with the members of the Teatime Reading Group, who are attempting to read through the entire list of Persephone Books. What dove-grey secrets would you like to unravel next?

Address 59 Lamb's Conduit Street, WC1N 3NB, Tel. +44(0)2072429292, www.persephonebooks.co.uk, info@persephonebooks.co.uk | Public Transport Piccadilly Line, Stop Russell Square | Opening Hours Mon–Fri 10am–6pm, Sat 12pm–5pm | Tip Visit the Lamb (94 Lamb's Conduit Street), a beautiful old-fashioned English pub named after William Lamb, who in 1577 brought clean water to the neighbourhood, hence the name Lamb's Conduit Street.

82 Playful Promises
Never out of knickers!

Boxpark in Shoreditch is a pop-up mall constructed of stripped and refitted shipping containers with a mixture of global and local shops. This is the home of lingerie shop Playful Promises.

Entering the small shop, you will see row upon row of colourful lacy bras, briefs, bodysuits and corsets. Venturing further inside, opposite the till you will encounter a statue of the Virgin Mary in a nun's habit, holding a pair of racy knickers. A neon sign above her head says: »Treat me gently, I'm a virgin«. Many people come in here just to photograph the statue!

For Emma Parker, the designer and owner of Playful Promises, it reflects the shop's identity: »Frivolous, flirty, and just a little bit dirty in that cheeky, quintessentially English way!« She has loved frilly, lacy underwear ever since she bought her first pair of fancy knickers at the age of eighteen. Her love for fabulous lingerie, which she amassed quite a large collection of, motivated her to design her own – also because she found the prices she had to pay for underwear seemed to get higher the smaller the item was. Therefore all the lingerie you can purchase here is very reasonably priced and suitable for both lingerie addicts and lingerie virgins.

Emma started the business in 2004. Her first boutique was on Brick Lane and she moved to Boxpark in 2011 because she liked the Boxpark initiative and the idea of a pop-up mall. Her customers are mostly female; a lot of them are East-End stylish young ladies with an interest in vintage. But Playful Promises are also happy to help and advise male customers buying gifts – or maybe something for themselves? Playful Promises designs two lingerie collections a year. Besides underwear, they also sell a range of retro swimwear, nightwear and dresses. Asked what she most enjoys about working at Playful Promises, Emma replies: »I can go for months without doing laundry and I never run out of clean knickers!«

Address Boxpark Unit 14, Bethnal Green Road, E1 6GY, Tel. +44(0)2077399217, www.playfulpromises.com, customerservices@playfulpromises.com | Public Transport Northern Line, Stop Old Street | Opening Hours Mon–Weds 11am–7pm, Thurs 11am–8pm, Fri-Sat 11am–7pm, Sun 12pm–6pm | Tip Discover the many other stylish shops in Boxpark!

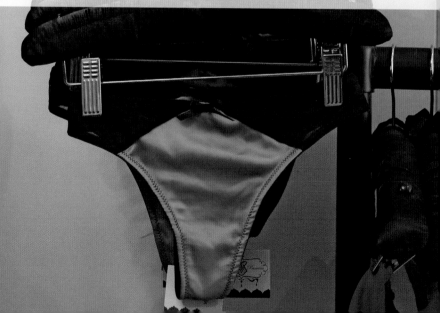

83 __ Postcard Teas
Tea culture in Dering Street

If you are in need of a little peace and quiet after the hustle and bustle of London's main shopping streets, why not head for Dering Street, a small cul-de-sac off Oxford Street. Here you will find Postcard Teas, where you can relax and sample a tea master's tea produced by Master Luo, Master Xu or other exceptional growers! The shop, famed for its calm and friendly atmosphere, sells loose tea from small farms, most of them under 15 acres.

Tim D'Offay, who fell in love with the beverage and its culture over 20 years ago, is the owner of the shop. For him, it is the only drink in the world that has its own growing, drinking and processing culture. He founded the first company to put the maker's name and location on all the teas and blends it sells. Today he and his team travel to 70 small producers in eight different countries all over Asia to source their exceptional products. The postcards that have given the shop its name were collected on these journeys. But there is also another application to them: customers can choose one, write a name and a message on it and the shop will send it together with their chosen tea to any destination in the world.

The choice is difficult, though: as most of us are no experts, how do you go about choosing the right blend? This is where Tim's long-standing expertise comes in. He and his knowledgeable colleagues will help you to make your choice. Why not try Master Matsumoto's Supernatural black tea, which is grown without any chemicals, herbicides, fertilisers or even manure? Or, if you want something really special, go for Master Luo's 2013 Firing King Prize Winning West Lake Long Jing. Only 150 grams of it have been produced in total! There's so much to learn about tea and if you want to deepen your knowledge, you can join one of Tim's weekly talks on Saturday mornings and immerse yourself in the culture of tea – tasting included!

POSTCARD TEAS

Address 9 Dering Street, New Bond Street, W1S 1AG, Tel. +44(0)2076293654, www.postcardteas.com, info@postcardteas.com | Public Transport Bakerloo, Central, Jubilee, Victoria Line, Stop Oxford Circus, Bond Street | Opening Hours Mon–Sat 10.30am–6.30pm | Tip The German composer Georg Friedrich Händel lived in nearby Brook Street. Visit his museum (25 Brook Street)!

OOLONG TEA

MASTER LIN'S GOLD MEDAL
MI GUA XIANG (HONEY BLOSSOM) 2012
This handmade Honey Blossom Phoenix
Oolong has received gold medals in Dan Cong
competitions. The tree is around 300 years old
and grows at 1200 meters on Mount Wu Dong.
In Spring 2012 it produced less than 4 kilos of
tea. Sugar-sweet with an intense floral, honeyed
flavour, this exceptional tea can be enjoyed
over 20-30 infusions if brewed with care.
10g Caddy £28.00
10g Refill only £25.00

84 Radio Days

A shop of her own

One of the remarkable things about Radio Days is its shop window. For owners Chrissie Layzell and Lee Williams, the window is a labour of love. The wonderful seasonal displays range from a 1920s speakeasy and a turquoise beachside picnic to Marilyn Monroe with her white skirts flying.

The attention to detail and the sense of storytelling that is so noticeable in the window display continues inside, too. Each carefully scripted area of the small mint-green shop with its pink back room tells a little story. There's a very serious man standing at a bar covered with champagne glasses and Magnum bottles, a figure in a beautiful vintage bathing suit is about to go on holiday, and collections of powder compacts, handbags, suitcases and shoes compete with old signs, magazines and chocolate boxes between glamorous feather boas and glittery glass necklaces.

In the back room, clothes racks are topped with mannequins' heads, making it look as if several well-dressed ladies are queuing here. Men have their own separate, more »manly« area decorated with signs, where scarves, hats, 1940s suits and coats are displayed. Radio Days sells vintage clothing, collectables and accessories from the 1920s to the 1980s, but the atmosphere of the shop reminds visitors of the glamour of the 1920s and 30s.

All this is the work of Chrissie and Lee, whose enthusiasm for vintage is tangible here. It all started in 1993 when Chrissie, who had a background in selling vintage clothing and worked a lot in other people's shops, decided she wanted her own shop. She was looking for a business close to home as she lived on the South Bank. Finally she found Radio Days with its beautiful art deco façade and was able to rent it cheaply. She started buying vintage clothes at boot fairs and markets and opened the business. At last, a shop of her own! Today, Radio Days enjoys quite a reputation: even Prince Charles came to visit it in 2012.

Address 87 Lower Marsh, SE1 7AB, Tel. +44(0)2079280800, www.radiodaysvintage.co.uk, radiodays@easy.com | **Public Transport** Bakerloo, Jubilee, Northern, Waterloo, City Line, Stop Waterloo | **Opening Hours** Mon–Sat 10am–6pm, Fri 10am–7pm | **Tip** You can choose between the Florence Nightingale Museum (2 Lambeth Palace Road) or the Garden Museum (5 Lambeth Palace Road). Go in the opposite direction if you would rather visit the London Fire Brigade Museum (94a, Southwark Bridge Road).

85 Retrouvius

New life for old things

Adam Hills and his wife Maria Speake established their architectural salvage and design business in 1993 in Glasgow. They had both studied architecture, and witnessing the demolition of Victorian buildings in the early 90s, they deemed it a waste of good materials. They founded both the salvage and the design company, which is run by Maria, because they wanted to show what could be done with salvaged stones, floors and fittings. Using reclaimed materials is not cheap because they need to be rescued and restored, and you also have to come up with inventive ways of integrating these pieces into modern environments: with too much salvage, your home will look like a junk shop! Adam and Maria are passionate about using old materials in a contemporary way so that they don't lose their character. For example, old science lab benches are turned into tabletops and glass funnels become lights.

In 2000, the couple moved to London and built up their business again here. Today, it occupies two buildings in Kensal Rise, a residential area in West London. 20 percent of the salvaged items are exported to Ireland, Germany, Switzerland or Japan. Many of the design customers are actors, directors and people working in the media. Adam and his team try to source in large quantities from clearances, schools, hospitals and offices. For example, they bought ¼ kilometer of shelving from the patent office, 1700 chairs from a school, 600 enamel lamps from a motor plant and 40 tables from a university.

One of Adam's favourite finds was 200 tons of Derbyshire stone salvaged from Heathrow Terminal Two. One evening he was chatting to a stonemason at a dinner party, who told him that the terminal was going to be demolished. He waited five years for the demolition to happen and finally was able to salvage the stone. In a very fitting coincidence, this stone – originally quarried on Chatsworth land – was later used to refurbish Chatsworth House.

Address 1016 Harrow Road, NW10 5 NS, Tel. +44(0)2089606060, www.retrouvius.com, mail@retrouvius.com | Public Transport Bakerloo Line, Stop Kensal Green | Opening Hours Mon–Sat 10am–6pm | Tip Walk to Kensal Green Cemetery, one of the finest cemeteries in London. Here are the graves of William Makepeace Thackeray, Charles Babbage and Harold Pinter among others.

86 __ Riders & Squires
Look the part

Are you a polo player, a rider or just horse crazy? Or are you simply looking for sturdy well-made leather boots? In all of these cases, this lovely old-fashioned shop in one of the small lanes behind Kensington High Street is well worth a visit. It is one of the few remaining shops in Central London catering for riders and polo players.

Riders and Squires sells saddles, bridles, hats, clothing, crops and whips for adults and children. You will find an extensive range of polo equipment here, from mallets to boots, belts and polo whites. The belts and many of the other products are made in Argentina, where everyone plays polo, rich and poor alike. As polo can be dangerous if players are not protected properly, you can also buy protective gear such as safety hats, face masks, gloves, goggles or kneepads.

Footwear ranges from short and long to light-weight boots, which are used in hot countries. If you never have played polo before, you may be asking yourself why all the horses are called ponies, even if they look rather big. The knowledgeable shop manager, Claire King, has the answer to this question: originally no horse higher than 54 inches was allowed to play in the game. Today this limit no longer applies, but smaller animals can move more swiftly and are thus often preferred.

Claire started to work in the shop eight years ago and has been riding horses herself since she was four years old. A lot of Riders and Squires' customers are regulars. Even if they don't ride in London, they keep horses at their country houses or go on riding holidays. Many come again and again to chat and buy new polo or riding equipment. »It's like having friends showing up every six months,« says Claire. She especially enjoys seeing the children grow up; some of them started playing polo when they were only four years old! So do you fancy taking up riding or polo playing? Even if not, after a visit to the shop you will at least be able to look the part!

Address 8 Thackeray Street, W8 5ET, Tel. +44 (0)2079374377, www.ridersandsquires.co.uk, info@ridersandsquires.co.uk | Public Transport Circle, District Line, Stop Kensington High Street | Opening Hours Mon–Fri 10am–2pm, 2.30pm–7pm, Sat 10am–2pm, 2.30pm–6pm | Tip Kensington Roof Gardens (99 Kensington High Street) with 6,000 square metres of themed gardens are free of charge and definitely worth a visit!

87 — Ruby Violet

Ice-cold dreams

Do you like ice cream? Who doesn't? However, shops or cafés dedicated to these cold delights are few and far between in London and you have to look hard to find one. Why is this – because people eat less ice cream here as it supposedly rains so much?

Julie Fisher, the owner of Ruby Violet, didn't care about the weather. She wanted to do something to enrich the life in Tufnell Park, the community where she lived. Motivated by her interest in food and cooking, she started experimenting with different ice cream recipes and had so much fun that she decided to open an ice cream parlour. In 2012 she founded Ruby Violet, which is named after her grandmother. In the shop the name is written in ruby-red neon letters above the counter. It has been a centre of communal life right from the beginning. Julie makes ice cream for birthdays, weddings and street parties as well as taking her ice-cream van to markets. Even if it rains cats and dogs, friends and neighbours meet here to try out new ice cream flavours, and will probably have a cup of coffee as well.

Fancy the sound of liquorice and blackcurrant? Lemon and cardamom? Basil? Pineapple and chili? Salted Caramel, Seville oranges and marmalade or Belgian Chocolate? These are only a few of the many ice cream and sorbet flavours Julie and her team create in the shop on a daily basis. They change the flavours according to season, using only fresh ingredients, organic milk and free-range eggs. In the summer, fruits are sourced locally if possible. Julie's passion for experimenting with different recipes not only resulted in an astonishing range of new ice cream flavours, she also wrote a book called »Ice Cream Dreams« with recipes for her amazing sweets.

Even if you don't live in Tufnell Park, you're very welcome to try them. Julie enjoys it if customers suggest new flavours to her – so what would your dream flavour be?

Address 18 Fortess Road, NW5 2HL, Tel. +44(0)2076090444, www.rubyviolet.co.uk, parlour@rubyviolet.co.uk | **Public Transport** Northern Line, Stop Kentish Town | **Opening Hours** Sat–Thurs 11am–7pm, Fri 11am–10pm | **Tip** The Forum (9–17 Highgate Road) is an art-deco style concert venue built as a cinema in 1934. Here you can listen to British and international music groups.

88 — The Sampler
Cheers, Ivy!

What sets The Sampler apart from other wine merchants is that you can try many of the wines here before you buy them. Jamie Hutchison, the managing director, founded the first shop with Dawn Mannis in Islington in 2006. Dawn handles the business's marketing side, whereas Jamie is responsible for financing and sourcing the wine. In 2010 they opened their second shop here in South Kensington.

They focus on wines sourced directly from small producers in different countries throughout Europe. They also stock a range of »Grower Champagne« from thirteen different growers. It's Jamie's job to visit the producers, something he enjoys it very much. For example, he might find a fantastic wine grown on a small remote farm in Northern Italy, and he will be able to sell it in The Sampler because of its unique business concept. They came up with this model when Jamie saw the sampling machines used by wineries in Greve in Chianti.

Usually customers who don't know a wine will go by brand or by price, but Jamie doesn't think these are good reasons to buy wine. The sampler machine allows customers to judge a wine by tasting it, which really should be the deciding factor. This gives Jamie the opportunity to buy and sell really good wine from small growers. There are ten sampling machines in each shop. A nitrogen blanket prevents oxygen from getting into the open wine bottles and keeps the wine fresh for up to three weeks. When you enter the shop, you first register and then you will be able to taste a variety of wines for a small fee. There are different machines for red wines, white wines and sweet wines. The bottles are rotated so that every wine sold in the shop can be tasted eventually. The Icon machine contains some of the most expensive and rare wines you usually couldn't afford to buy per bottle.

And there is another thing that sets The Sampler apart: the shop dog Ivy, who loves to chase corks. Cheers, Ivy!

Address 35 Thurloe Place, SW7 2HP, Tel. +44(0)2072255091, www.thesampler.co.uk, jamie@thesampler.co.uk | Public Transport Circle, District, Piccadilly Line, Stop South Kensington | Opening Hours Mon–Sat 11.30am–10pm, Sun 11.30am–7pm | Tip Sit outside one of the many cafés or restaurants on Exhibition Road and enjoy the street life!

89 __ Scarlet & Violet

Relaxed and natural

Scarlet & Violet in Kensal Rise is probably one of the busiest flower shops in London. If you come to the store in the morning, there is hardly any room to move: wherever you look, you will see beautiful flowers in vintage enamel jugs taking up every last bit of free space. Amid this symphony of colours and shapes, the shop's owner Victoria Brotherson and her team of florists are busily moving about, creating the beautiful bouquets and flower arrangements the shop is known for. It's a good idea to let them choose the flowers for you, because there is such an abundance here that you simply won't be able to decide: do you want bundles of pompom-headed hydrangeas in pastels, or a jewel-coloured mixture of dahlias and cosmea? You might end up taking them all!

The floral arrangements focus on traditional seasonal blooms and look like something you could have picked straight from your own garden – provided that you're the proud owner of an extensive cut flower garden, of course! »Most of our customer are a varied bunch of locals,« says Victoria, but quite a few stars and celebrities – such as Kate Moss, who chose Victoria as her wedding florist – have also discovered this amazing shop. The team of eight working here now provides flowers for up to two to three weddings a week and many other major events throughout the year, as well as selling around 350 flower bouquets a week. A florist can't sleep in: the day starts at 4.30, early enough to source flowers at New Covent Garden Market.

Although all this is very hard work, Victoria wouldn't change her job for anything. She enjoys it hugely, especially working together with her two sisters who are also part of the team: »We have a fantastic time, making my life very easy – hilarious stories keep us entertained.« Prior to opening the shop in 2006, Victoria had already worked with flowers for 14 years. With Scarlet & Violet, she has fulfilled her dream of creating flower arrangements that are both relaxed and natural.

Address 76 Chamberlayne Road, NW10 3JJ, Tel +44(0)2089699446, www.scarletandviolet.com, info@scarletandviolet.co.uk | **Public Transport** Stop Kensal Rise, London Overground towards Stratford | **Opening Hours** Mon–Sat 8.30am–6pm | **Tip** Relax in nearby Queen's Park, which has a lot of sport facilities and a pet's corner including small goats for children.

90 The School of Life
Feeling better now?

Here you can purchase calm, bravery and kindness, learn how to carry your emotional baggage or focus for fifteen minutes on what really matters; this is not a church, temple or enchanted forest, but a shop: The School of Life shop. It was founded by Alain de Botton, a Swiss author and essayist who has dedicated his work and life to developing a »philosophy of everyday life«. He has written a series of self-help guides and several books on sex, love, travel, literature, philosophy and architecture.

In 2008, the School of Life opened in a small shop on Marchmont Street. In the basement they offer classes to improve every aspect of your life from beginning to end. Events, courses and classes range from »Finding a career that fits«, »How to balance work with life« and »How to worry less about money« to »How to make love last« and »How to face death«. The workshops and classes are taught by leading philosophers, scientists, artists, writers or other experts in different areas. They also offer one-to-one conversations with highly qualified therapists that can be booked as needed, like a dentist's appointment. Companies or individuals can also hold staff training sessions here.

In the shop on the ground floor you will find comfy chairs, calming grey walls and a grove of real silver birch trunks, all designed by Susanna Edwards and Joseph Harries. This is where you can buy your »Tools for Thinking«: a glass timer gives you 15 minutes to think about what really matters. Virtue dolls from Japan embody kindness, bravery or calm. Utopian candles remind you of an ideal world. You can also purchase notebooks dedicated to the school of thought you can relate to: if you're frightened, choose the Existentialist notebooks; if you view the world black in black, go for the Pessimist! Never know what to talk about when you meet someone? A toolkit for conversations with hundred questions will help you! Feeling a bit better now?

91__SCIN Gallery

Material worlds

Attached to the shop window is a sign saying »Fondle + Squeeze, the materials library«, making you extremely curious about what lies behind! Materials are not sold here, but instead can be touched, handled or hired – mostly in the form of samples. If you want to visit the gallery, you pay a fee and one of their interior and materials experts will accompany you through the four floors and try to find a material suitable to your needs.

Whether you are a designer or an architect, whether you want to use unusual materials in your house or outside, or whether you just love materials, it is definitely worth coming here to rummage through or hire a sample of the most innovative »stuff« in the world. Most of the time you just wonder how any of it can exist at all.

Take the stretchy concrete which can be knitted into surfaces or shapes, granite that is ground and mixed with yeast bacteria and becomes nearly as malleable as clay, or a meta-material called »acoustic cloak« that allows certain sound waves to pass and inhibits others. Other surfaces don't show fingermarks, concrete becomes translucent, wood luminous, and ceramics can be woven – everything is possible! The SCIN Gallery – by the way, SCIN is pronounced »skin«, nothing do with sin! – sources materials for every conceivable surface inside and outside buildings.

The founders Annabel Filer and Graham Cox, both designers and architects, wanted to bring new materials to the consumer and the best way was to showcase them and bring producers and designers/architects together. The gallery recently moved to Clerkenwell, now London's leading design district. Here Annabel organises changing exhibitions on the four gallery floors. The space is also hired out to companies looking for new materials or to Feng Shui experts doing workshops. It's easy to get excited about all the possibilities; take a dip into the world of new materials!

Address Morelands, 27 Old Street, EC1V 9HL, Tel. +44(0)2073577574, www.scin.co.uk, info@scin.co.uk | Public Transport Circle, Hammersmith, Metropolitan Line, Stop Barbican | Opening Hours open by appointment only | Tip Bunhill Fields Burial Ground (38 City Road) has a long history and contains the graves of William Blake, Daniel Defoe, John Bunyan and Susannah Wesley.

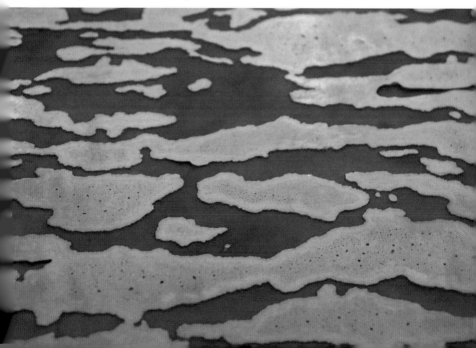

92___Second Nature
Vintage Gardening

This wonderful shop ticks several boxes at once. Beautiful plants: yes; vintage pots and gardening tools: yes; old gardening books: yes; anything else a gardener and vintage lover might like: definitely a yes! It sells gardening gifts, but the combination of gardening and vintage is what makes it so attractive.

The narrow Edwardian space with its beautiful curved shop window provides the perfect backdrop to whatever wonderful objects owner Richard Parker can find. Richard started out working for a garden design company. Because he loved old things, he rented their top floor and started to sell his own stuff there. Later he set up a shop in Highgate, moving his business to Muswell Hill in 2007.

Basically Richard buys whatever he's interested in himself: »I like to buy things I like without hoarding them at home and I don't mind selling them after a while in the shop.« Sometimes he also buys things with a specific customer in mind, which usually works out well too! For the antiques he goes to fairs and auctions in England, although the items he sources are not necessarily produced here.

There are for example German Kaiser lamps, which are very popular, Swedish ceramics or unused 1950s picnic sets. He also has a whole collection of 1950s clocks and alarm clocks, old vases, mirrors, cups and the occasional piece of furniture like a shelf, desk or display case. He likes illustrated natural history books, so he always has some of them in stock as well. Besides plants, the shop also sells other new things every gardener longs to have, like the wonderful silk scarves made in England with either fruit fly, worm or wasp patterns; beautiful clay pots, some tools, plant soaps or watering cans. In between this eclectic mixture there are some wonderful finds to make, like the wooden Noah's ark or an old rattle. Perhaps you've now been inspired to take up vintage gardening yourself?

Address 79 Fortis Green Road, N10 3HP, Tel. +44(0)2084441717, naturesecond@yahoo.com | **Public Transport** Northern Line, Stop East Finchley, then bus 102 to Muswell Hill Road | **Opening Hours** Mon 11am–4.30pm, Tues–Sat 9am–6pm, Sun 11am–4.30pm | **Tip** Have a salad at Chriskitch (7a Tetherdown). This deli has an Australian chef and does excellent food.

93__Sh!

Experts in women's sensuality

Sh! is the UK's first female-focused sex shop. Many years ago, Kathryn Hoyle visited some sex shops in Soho and found the experience both distasteful and alienating. The atmosphere was sleazy, the sex toys were ugly, and her feeling was that women weren't being catered for in the sex industry. This set her thinking and the result was Sh!, which Kathryn opened in 1992 using only seven hundred pounds and a can of pink paint. Kathryn wanted to create a safe space where women could enjoy browsing through erotic products without fear or worry.

A lot of the women who come here have never been to a sex shop before. Some suffer from emotional or physical issues and are referred by their GPs or therapists. While different forms of sexual expression, including bondage and spanking, have become more acceptable, many women still feel that they need permission to come to a sex shop. Sh! wants to help them to take charge of their own sexuality. Gentlemen, although not excluded, are asked to come in the company of a female friend or on Gents Night (Tuesdays 6–8pm).

The range of sex toys is crucial to the shop: Kathryn and her team are convinced that sex toys are just that – toys – and therefore should be pretty and playful, not ugly. Sh! has developed its own luxury brand of dildos, strap-ons, harnesses and bondage kits in different colours, shapes and sizes. Ever since »Sex and the City« rabbit vibrators have been very popular and »50 Shades of Grey« has led to a rise in purchases of love balls, which provide stimulation and strengthen the pelvic floor muscles, resulting in stronger orgasms. Whether straight, gay, bi- or transsexual, the Sh! team treads all women's sexuality as equal. They also hold readings of erotic literature and run erotic classes ranging from »Spanking« to »Blow his mind«. Sh! girls go through a six-month training period, enabling them to give advice whatever the client's different needs and preferences may be.

Address 57 Hoxton Square, N1 6PB, Tel. +44(0)2076135458, www.sh-womenstore.com, shop@sh-womenstore.com | **Public Transport** Northern Line, Stop Old Street | **Opening Hours** Mon–Sun 12pm–8pm | **Tip** Hoxton Square became a fashionable neighbourhood and a centre for the arts and media scene in the 1990s. If you want to watch trendy East Londoners, sit down on one of the park benches for a while.

94 Shepherds Falkiners
Love of paper

Paper nerds, listen up: this is a shop you can't miss! Shepherds Falkiners stocks decorative and fine art paper as well as bookbinding materials. It was originally two shops. Falkiners was founded in the 70s by Gabriel Falkiner and sold very fine decorative paper, whereas Shepherds is a bookbinding and conservation company run by Rob Shepherd. Their fusion in 2003/2004 resulted in the beautiful shop in Gillingham Street near Victoria Station, where you can indulge yourself with Japanese paper or take bookbinding courses.

Talking of Japanese paper, the range in the shop is second to none: Chiyogami paper, screen printed by hand and based on kimono designs from the Edo period, or Katazome-shi, meaning stencil-dyed paper, with its intense colours and patterns are only a few examples. »We import most of the Japanese paper via Canada,« explains shop manager Matthew Phillips, »because Rob Shepherd built up some contacts there over the years.« Besides Japanese paper, Shepherds Falkiners also sells marbled paper – the designs by the English artist Jemma Lewis are especially beautiful –, Nepalese paper, and paper designed by Rob Shepherd himself. If you don't know what to do with your paper, rest assured there are a million different possibilities. Apart from obvious uses like gift-wrapping or box making, fashion designers use paper from the shop to make paper dresses and interior designers use it as wallpaper. »There's not one type of customer« says Matthew, »literally everyone buys paper!«

On the bookbinding side of the business, you can purchase different kinds of leather from calf to reindeer, silks, linens, vellums, parchment and all the other materials you need for bookmaking and binding. The company also does restoration and book conservation, working with museums and private customers: does your family bible need restoring? And if all that is not enough for you, how about a bookbinding course, a calligraphy workshop or trying your hand at Japanese kite making? Are you ready to indulge in your love of paper?

Address 30 Gillingham Street, SW1V 1HU, Tel. +44 (0)2072339999, www.store.falkiners.com | Public Transport Circle, District, Victoria Line, Stop Victoria | Opening Hours Mon–Fri 10am–6pm, Sat 10am–5pm | Tip The Tate Britain is a short walk away and always worth a visit.

95 — The Spice Shop
Spice up your life

Can you tell the difference between saffron from India and saffron from Iran? Would you like to know what »Black Lava Salt« is? If you want to buy or find out more about spices, the Spice Shop in Blenheim Crescent near Portobello Road is the place for you.

This small yellow shop first opened its doors in 1995 but its story began before then when Birgit Erath, who was doing a degree in Business Studies, decided to look for a project to supplement her income. She started with a market stall and four spices and ploughed all of her profit into expanding her offer. She mixed the herbs and spices to create her own recipes and her reputation as a spice trader grew. Today the shop sells 2500 different spices and ships them to customers all over the world. It has also become an institution on Portobello Road Market and is often frequented by chefs and famous TV cooks seeking inspiration for their dishes. Four years ago Philip Erath, Birgit's son, took over the business in London and has recently opened another shop in Brighton. The spice blends are still mixed by Birgit Erath, who has moved back to a small town in Germany where the warehouse is located.

Philip will help you to choose from the huge selection of herbs, spices and blends. A learned chef, he is very knowledgeable about his products. You definitely need his advice if you don't know what »Throubi«, »Grains of Paradise«, or »Tonquin Beans« are. He also is always happy to suggest ideas for recipes and recommend the best spice for the dish you want to cook. For example, you could try »Cuban Adobo blend« to season grilled meat, soups or stews; add »Hackfleisch Gewürzmischung« to mince or flavour rice with »Persian Sabzi Polo«. One of Philip's favourite blends is »Raz al Hanout«, a Moroccan spice mix containing between 49 and 57 different ingredients. Use it in a tagine or stew, and your guests will crown you the master chef! If you haven't discovered your favourite spice yet, this is where you will find it.

MOROCCAN RAZ EL HANOUT

MOROCCAN TAGINE MIX

MOROCCAN CHICKEN SEASONING

MOROCCAN FISH SEASONING

MADRAS CURRY MEDIUM

MADRAS CURRY HOT

VINDALOO CURRY

ROGAN JOSH MILD

KASHMIRI MASALA

KASHMIRI FISH MASALA

PILI PILI

BOMBAY POTATO MIX

DAN MAS

THAI GREEN CURRY

THAI RED CURRY

MASSAMAN CURRY

RENDANG CURRY

SATAY MIX

NASI GORENG

JUNGLE CURRY

BURMESE CHICKEN CURRY

Address 1 Blenheim Crescent, W11 2EE, Tel. +44(0)2072214448, www.thespiceshop.co.uk, info@thespiceshop.co.uk | Public Transport Central, District, Circle Line, Stop Notting Hill Gate | Opening Hours Tues–Sat 9.30am–6pm, Sun 11am–4pm | Tip Go to Books for Cooks (4 Blenheim Crescent) and find some recipes for your spices!

96__Stanfords
Map the future

Edward Stanford, a London cartographer and map seller, lived in a world of rapid change and technological advancement. When he opened Stanford in 1853, no accurate map of London existed. Stanford appointed a team of surveyors and the resulting map of London was praised by the Royal Geographical Society »as the most perfect map of London that has ever been issued«. During his lifetime he witnessed exceptional discoveries of hitherto unknown territories, such as the exploration of Antarctica by Amundsen and Scott – he had a lively correspondence with the latter about maps – and helped to change our perception of the world by mapping it.

In 1947, Stanfords came into the hands of the Scottish cartographer Georg Philip and Son and focused on becoming one of the most important map retailers in the world. Today it is a leading all-round travel specialist. The floors in its famous shop in Covent Garden, which opened as a showroom in 1901, are covered in maps: the ground floor features the National Geographic map of the world, the first floor the National Geographic map of the Himalayas, centered on Everest, and the basement is covered by a giant A–Z map of central London. The ground floor café offers tired travellers the perfect place to relax. Besides maps from all over the world, Stanford also sells globes, travel literature, guides, reprints of historic maps and replicas of travel furniture and clothing.

For managing director Tony Maher, the challenges Stanfords faces in the era of Google maps, GPS and e-books are not daunting, but exciting. Edward Stanford faced similar challenges in his own time and Tony sees him as a source of inspiration, an incentive for the business to branch out into all areas related to travel. One unique service the shop already offers is a close-up map of an area and time of your choice – perhaps a detailed map of your birth place at the time of your birth! In future, the world will be mapped in increasingly personal terms.

Address 12–14 Long Acre, WC2E 9LP, Tel. +44(0)2078361321, www.stanfords.co.uk, sales@stanfords.co.uk | **Public Transport** Northern, Piccadilly Line, Stop Covent Garden, Leicester Square | **Opening Hours** Mon–Fri 9am–8pm, Sat 10am–8pm, Sun 12pm–6pm | **Tip** The London Transport Museum (Covent Garden Piazza) is worth a visit.

97 St Martins Models

A Lamborghini for 100 pounds

Have you always dreamed of a Lamborghini but never had enough money to make your dream come true? Laurence Lambert, the manager of St Martins Models, will make it possible. The shop is located in Cecil Court, a small pedestrian street near Covent Garden, which is often used as a location for films. Cecil Court is a paradise for collectors: antiquarians for children's books, antique shops, collectors' shops specialising in coins, paper money and medals or jewellery – every shop here covers a special area of collecting. Coffeehouse chains are not permitted.

St Martins Models is the only shop for model cars still existing in London and thus a prime destination for collectors of miniature automobiles. The shop opened in 2011 to support Diecast Legends, a thriving online business. They wanted to give collectors the opportunity to pick up and feel the models before buying them. Who collects model cars? Children, for example, and the shop stocks models that collectors with only a little pocket money are able to afford. However, most of the »children« who enter the shop are actually adults: anybody who loves racing cars or has owned a racing car at one point in their lives. Many people who come here own an Aston Martin, a Ferrari or even a Renault 14 and are looking for a miniature version of their car.

You might bump into the American talkshow host Jay Leno or another car-crazy celebrity. Like real cars, model automobiles come in all colours and shapes. If they are very rare or special in any other regard, they quickly become very sought-after collectors' items and rise in value up to several hundred pounds. Laurence Lambert distinguishes between two types of collectors: some of them buy a model hoping its value will go up and they'll be able to sell it for a better price. Others develop an emotional connection to the object and just think it's great to be able to own a Lamborghini Countach for 100 pounds!

Address 15 Cecil Court, WC2N 4EZ, Tel. +44(0)2074978157, www.stmartinsmodels.co.uk | Public Transport Northern, Piccadilly Line, Stop Leicester Square | Opening Hours Mon–Fri 10am–6.30pm, Sat 10am–6pm, Sun 2pm–6pm | Tip There are several »blue plaques« in Cecil Court to remind visitors of important events and inhabitants. One such inhabitant was Mozart, who stayed here 1764 at the house of a barber.

98 SugarSin

18 pounds of sweets

Who doesn't remember the scene in Pippi Longstocking where she goes to a sweet shop with a suitcase full of gold coins and buys sweets for all the children in the village?

This scene stayed with Josefin Deckel and Anna Nielsen, two sisters from Sweden who came to London six years ago to study. It inspired them to open SugarSin after they realised there was a definite shortage of good sweet shops in London. It took two years until the shop was finally able to open its doors in Long Acre, Covent Garden. The walls with their bright sweet colours, stripes and rhombuses create a fantastic background for the multi-coloured jewels displayed here: Blueberry-Vanilla Bumlings, Kryptonites, Gunpowder Frogs, Salted Caramels, Witches' screams, Filidutter, Almond Caramel Lollipops, Raspberry Liquorice Diamonds … and they're all edible! Josefin's favourite sweets are liquorice with raspberry – or is it blueberry vanilla? The problem is that it is too difficult to decide!

Many of the sweets in the shop naturally come from Sweden, like the salty liquorice fish, a popular Swedish treat. Anna and Josefin's main goal is to sell sweets that taste good. That's why they stock sweets from all over Europe, including English classics like Sherbet Lemons or Pear Drops. For Anna and Josefin the quality of the sweets is also very important. They try to avoid artificial colours, except for blue bonbons, and all their goods are free of genetically modified ingredients. If Josefin and Anna can't find something they just make it themselves. They already stock a whole range of home-made lollipops with apple, almond, caramel and coconut flavours. They change their selection of sweets depending on the season. In the winter they sell chocolate treats and sweets containing spices; in the summer a lot of them are fruit flavoured.

If you're drooling now, don't worry: you can buy some sweets – even 18 pounds of them like Pippi!

ndmade
pple Lollie
£1

Address 70 Long Acre, WC2E 9JS, Tel. +44(0)2072409994, sugarsin.co.uk, hello@sugarsin.co.uk | Public Transport Piccadilly Line, Stop Covent Garden | Opening Hours Mon–Sat 10.30am–8pm, Sun 12pm–6pm | Tip Are you a dancer or interested in ballet? In nearby Drury Lane there are several excellent ballet shops.

99___This Shop Rocks
Anything Strange

There are many vintage outlets in Brick Lane, but This Shop Rocks is something special. Established in 2007, the shop sells an eclectic mixture of vintage clothes, hats, books, porcelain, stuffed animals, model ships, dolls, and countless other weird and wonderful items. You will need to take your time when you come here, because on every surface and in every corner of the shop you are sure to find something interesting.

Doesn't the wooden little cow on wheels look like she needs a new home? The lamp with a Chinese porcelain figure as a base would look really good on grandma's couch table, and that Edwardian wedding dress is just so beautiful! When you have looked your fill upstairs, go downstairs and start all over again with books, clothes and porcelain.

Sandy and Candy Sanderson, who own the family business, have a long history of buying, selling and making things. They both have an art school background, did studio pottery, weaving, taught art in schools, ran a riding school and travelled all over the world. They always bought and sold antiques, which finally led them to open the shop in Brick Lane they run with their son Timothy.

Sandy makes hats, regarding them as sculptures you can wear. When he and Candy were young, they wore a lot of vintage clothes from Edwardian times or from the 1920s: »Wearing clothes of your forebears is a natural thing for young people.« He also loves wind-up gramophones and jazz records, of which they have several in the shop. Candy favours dolls and toys, which populate most chairs and free surfaces in the store, but she also will purchase old model ships or stuffed animals if she can get her hands on them. If she finds something very special it is sometimes difficult for her to part with it and she holds onto it just a little bit longer. When asked what her reasons are for choosing something for the shop, she just shrugs her shoulders and says: »Anything strange!«

Address 129–131 Brick Lane, E1 6RU, Tel. +44(0)2077397667, info@thisshoprocks.co.uk | Public Transport Circle, District, Hammersmith Line, Stop Aldgate East | Opening Hours Mon–Sun 11am–6pm | Tip Brick Lane Market is open on Sundays from 9am–5pm.

100__ Tomfoolery

To someone you love

Tomfoolery is a jewellery shop every bride is sure to love. During the wedding season, the light and spacious shop in the centre of Muswell Hill dedicates an entire section of its gallery to bridal jewellery. They offer a wide selection of designer pieces, ranging from engagement rings, wedding and eternity rings to gifts from bridesmaids to groomsmen.

They have even thought of the groom's cufflinks and something for the mother of the bride! Using their bespoke service, you can have a one-of-a-kind engagement ring or wedding bands made. Their in-house expert will advise you on the materials, engravings and gemstones you can choose and will guide you through the process. But you don't have to be a bride or groom to have something made for you – why not design something for your children, parents, friends or even yourself? Tomfoolery not only sells bridal gems and baubles, they also offer a range of contemporary designer jewellery, showcasing a selection of each designer's work in separate cases in their gallery.

They stock well-known makers such as Jane Adams, Disa Allsopp, Ruth Tomlinson or Polly Wales. Around 70 percent of the designers are British, the rest come from all over the world. Laura Kay, who manages the family business today, visits trade shows in Paris, New York and Munich to source all the pieces. Laura's parents Nicky and Peter Kay started the shop in 1984 in a much smaller store two doors down the road.

Ten years ago Tomfoolery moved to its current premises. Laura started working in the shop during the holidays when she was 15. She then took a degree in photography and was a stylist for Hermès before returning to her roots. She loves working here because for her, jewellery creates a special connection between the person who gives it and the one who receives it. »Jewellery is not like any other thing you sell. It is very personal and has emotional attachment to it. You give a piece of jewellery to someone you really love.«

Address 109 Fortis Green Road, N10 3HP, Tel. +44(0)2084447000, http://tomfoolerylondon.co.uk, info@tomfoolerylondon.co.uk | Public Transport Northern Line, Stop East Finchley, then bus 102 to Muswell Hill Road | Opening Hours Mon – Sat 9.30am – 5.30pm | Tip A walk to Alexandra Palace (Alexandra Palace Way) takes a while, but will reward you with one of the best views in London!

101___Toye, Kenning & Spencer

The Grand Master's apron

Toye, Kenning & Spencer makes and sells »identity wear« – although this trendy expression does not do justice to the craftsmanship and range of fascinating products that Toye, Kenning and Spencer create. The company produces Masonic regalia, works for the royal household and the police force, creates gift ranges for OBEs and also carries out commissions for societies and associations. Toye manufactures medals, ribbons, embroidery, uniforms, badges, cufflinks, jewellery and much more besides. The business has two manufacturing sites: in Birmingham, all the metal is manufactured, including stamping, enamelling and engraving. The Bedworth factory is where the company does its weaving of ribbons, embroidery, braids and laces.

Freddy Toye recently started to work for the business, and as a member of the founder family he is very interested in its history. It all started with his ancestor Guillaume Henry Toyé, a Huguenot who had to leave France in 1685. After his arrival in Britain, he took up the family business of weaving, lace making and embroidery once more – and thrived. Over the years, Toye merged with other companies. The Toye family and their business have strong links with Freemasonry: Masonic regalia provided the company's bread and butter for many years and continue to play an important role today. In fact, the shop employees have to be Masons, as Masonic regalia are so diverse that insider knowledge is required to provide good customer service.

But even if you're not a Mason, you can still come here to improve your knowledge of Freemasonry or buy gifts and accessories from the shop. On the first floor Toye has a clubroom where a Masonic lodge meets once a month. Here you can find a beautiful collection of Masonic museum pieces in glass cases; one of the most interesting is the apron made by Toye, Kenning & Spencer for the first Grand Master of Germany after World War II.

Address 19–21 Great Queen Street, WC2B 5BE, Tel. +44(0)2072420471, www.toye.com, info@toye.com | **Public Transport** Central, Piccadilly Line, Stop Holborn | **Opening Hours** Mon–Fri 9am–5.30pm, Sat 9am–3pm | **Tip** Opposite the shop you'll find the English Freemasons' headquarters in an imposing 1930s art deco building. The museum houses many Masonic artifacts and is free of charge.

102 — Treadwell's Books

A meeting of minds

»A bookshop is a sanctuary for the mind.« These words appear on a sign in the shop window of Treadwell's Books in Store Street. The bookshop sells antiquarian and new esoteric and occult books as well as books on anthropology, cultural history, religion and beliefs from all over the world. Not only does Treadwell's specialise in Pagan religion, Wicca and witchcraft; it also hosts a series of academic lectures by scholars from Oxford or Cambridge specialised in ancient magical manuscripts, bringing them together with people who actually practice these spells.

Christina Oakley Harrington, the founder of Treadwell's, trained and worked as an academic historian for 15 years. At the age of 40 she decided on a change of career and revived the occult bookshop tradition in Central London – a tradition that dates back to around 1800 – opening Treadwell's in 2003. Through her upbringing in West Africa, Christina developed an early interest in magic and tribal religions, which led her to become a Pagan. As an academic historian, she also knows how to give the occult a scholarly side. This makes her the ideal person to bring the academic and magic worlds together.

One of her many stories recounts how Irving Finkel, a curator at the British Museum specialised in Mesopotamian languages and cultures, gave a talk on Mesopotamian demons at Treadwell's. He talked about the diseases caused by the demons and what spells the priests used to speak to the dead. He concluded his lecture by saying: »I'm told that there are still people who do séances to speak to the spirits of the dead, but nobody has ever invited me to one; so if anybody does them in the audience and cares to invite me, I would love to speak to them afterwards.« Sure enough, after the lecture some members of the audience came up to him, invited him to a séance and asked for advice about rituals and the wording of spells. For Christina Oakley Harrington, these exchanges of the mind are perhaps the most important reason she opened the bookshop.

Address 33 Store Street, WC1E 7BS, Tel. +44(0)2074198507, www.treadwells-london.com, info@treadwells-london.com | **Public Transport** Northern Line, Stop Goodge Street | **Opening Hours** Mon–Fri 1pm–5pm, Sat, Sun 12pm–7pm | **Tip** Visit Pollock's Toy Museum (1 Scala Street) with its toy theatres, dolls and mechanical toys.

103 Vintage Heaven
A shop like a garden

Margaret Willis's life has been as colourful as the cups, plates and saucers she sells in her shop in Columbia Road. She started out in Ireland working for the Northern Ireland Civil Service, emigrated to Canada, returned to Belfast and found employment in a nursery, moved to London as a social worker, got married and had a family, took a three-year course in horticulture and taught organic gardening and garden design.

She is also a practising Buddhist, active member of the Green Party (even once standing for her local constituency as an MEP) and an avid collector of old things with two garages full of stuff. Whenever posters or leaflets had to be printed for a campaign, she organised a jumble sale and raised the money. In 2007 she finally opened Vintage Heaven: »My Buddhist practice, my jumble saleing and my belief that we must not waste resources all came together in this shop.« This philosophy is also reflected in the way her shop is organised. Margaret applies the same principles here as she does in gardening. Things are kept simple, limiting one area to a particular colour: everything blue goes together, as does everything green, everything pink, everything yellow; black and white go together with red. These blocks of colour create a feeling of abundance. The background is white, which lifts everything up. She only ever buys what she likes, be it Poole Pottery or well-designed and functional Woods Wear from Stoke-on-Trent in green, yellow or blue.

The shop and the little Cakehole Café in the back are only open on two days a week: Saturday is for the locals and Sunday is the big business day, as everyone is here for the Columbia Road Flower Market. Every three weeks Margaret rearranges all her crockery and the other items she sells. To keep the energy of the pieces, everything needs to be cleaned and dusted – which takes time: her husband even once asked her if she had a lover because she was so busy with the shop. A shop like a garden is a lot of work!

Address 82 Columbia Road, E2 7QB, Tel. +44(0)1277215968 | **Public Transport** Central Line, Stop Bethnal Green | **Opening Hours** Sat 12pm–6pm, Sun 8.30am–5.30pm | **Tip** You have to come here on a Sunday and experience the unique Columbia Road Flower Market!

104__The VIVOBAREFOOT Experience

Discover your potential

Vivobarefoot is not your usual shoe shop, but you'll only discover this if you take a closer look. At first glance, the shoes here look similar to the footwear you can find in any other shoe shop – everything from running shoes to wellies – but if you look closely at them you will see that they are wider and more flexible than normal shoes and have a much thinner sole. Nadine Horn, who works here as a barefoot coach, explains why: »Because we wear shoes, our brain doesn't know any more what happens under our feet. We've lost the direct contact to the ground, which changes the way we stand, walk or run. With shoes we walk differently than we would walk naturally. We don't have enough space for movement and as a result we don't know how to use the evolutionary masterpiece called foot anymore!« Masterpiece indeed – did you know that we have 200,000 nerve ends in our feet?

The barefoot running guru Lee Saxby helped to develop Vivobarefoot's shoes, which don't change the natural movements of your feet. The width and softness of the shoes guarantee that your feet have enough space to move, and an insulating layer in the sole makes sure that no sharp objects will hurt your feet. Nadine knows from her own experience that the wrong footwear can lead to health problems. She took part in a triathlon but had problems with the running part. With a swollen knee and hamstring, she had to give up. When she heard Vivobarefoot's motto »Running is a skill« it immediately made sense to her and she started her training as a barefoot coach. The shop primarily sells a concept. Many people come here with health problems caused by wearing the wrong footwear. You can test your »walking skills« here and book a course where you learn how to stand, walk or run naturally. For Nadine, her work is a kind of research. As a barefoot coach she set out to find her human potential and wants to help others to discover theirs.

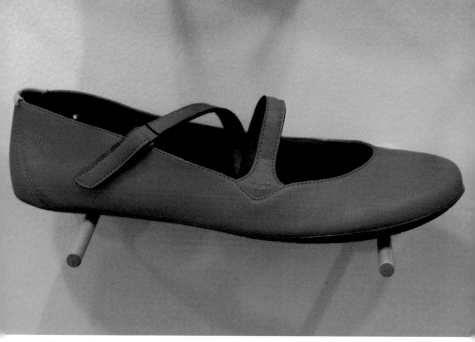

Address 64 Neal Street, WC2H, Tel. +44(0)2073795959, www.vivobarefoot.com, customerservices@vivobarefoot.com | Public Transport Piccadilly Line, Stop Covent Garden | Opening Hours Mon–Sat 10.30am–7pm, Sun 12pm–6pm | Tip If you are a coffee aficionado, try Monmouth (27 Monmouth Street) for excellent coffee roasted in Bermondsey.

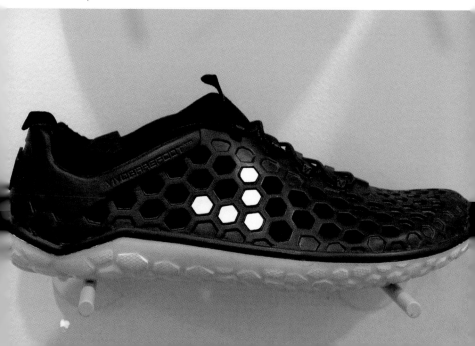

105 __ VV Rouleaux

Fur trims for cats and flowers for the Queen

Why are ribbons, trimmings or silk flowers so appealing? Because they just are! On entering VV Rouleaux, many customers – most of them are female – will breathe a deep sigh of happiness and immediately start to rummage through narrow strips of fabric – something that can go on for hours! No-one knows what causes this attraction, but it must be deeply ingrained in the female psyche.

The shop has the most wonderful collection of ribbons, ranging from velvet, silk, satin, grosgrain, wire edge, organdy, striped, spotted, gingham and tartan – not to forget the trimmings, which include handmade Spanish tassels, bullions, braids, fringes, cords and so on … suffice it to say that they do hats and headdresses, silk flowers and corsages and furniture trimmings as well. Particularly lovely are small flowers made from pipe cleaners in the Czech Republic.

The owner of the shop, Annabel Lewis, trained as a florist but was disappointed by the lack of beautiful ribbons for her flower bouquets. She opened VV Rouleaux in 1990. The business's reputation grew, it won several awards and today many fashion and interior designers are regular customers. It first opened in Parsons Green, moved several times and is now located in Marylebone Lane. The products are sourced from all over the world, but VV Rouleaux also offers bespoke ribbons and various factories produce for them in large quantities.

Brides can order bespoke headdresses; or what about a bespoke Venetian-style mask? You can even make your own headdress (if you don't know how, sign up for one of the courses they offer)! If by now you have already bought far too many ribbons and trimmings, rest assured that you are not the first one to be seduced by the beauty of the shop and its contents. In fact, VV Rouleaux once had a request to make a diamanté fur-trimmed invitation – sent to cats for a cat's birthday party! Even the Queen has yielded to the shop's temptation and had a flower bouquet for one of her hats made here.

Address 102 Marylebone Lane, W1U 2QD, Tel. +44(0) 2072245179, vvrouleaux.com, marylebone@vvrouleaux.com | **Public Transport** Central, Jubilee Line, Stop Bond Street | **Opening Hours** Mon–Sat 9.30am–6pm, Weds 10.30am–6pm, Thurs 9.30am–6.30pm | **Tip** The British Dental Association Museum (64 Wimpole Street) houses over 20,000 items to do with dentistry in the UK. Why not buy one of their molar mugs?

VVRouleaux *Atelier*

www.vvrouleaux.com

Flowers fit for a Queen !!!

106___Vx
Vegan and cool

This shop is called Vegan Cross because it is close to King's Cross station, conveniently located for vegan travellers from the UK and abroad. It has become a tourist destination in its own right for the vegan community. Here you can get everything a vegan needs: from t-shirts, bags, hats, shoes, purses and stickers to groceries like sausages, cheese, energy bars and chocolate spread. They also sell homemade vegan sandwiches, toasties, wraps and cupcakes. Vx even stocks vegan cookbooks!

Everyone who works in the shop is vegan and very passionate about the products. Many customers suffer from food allergies or rare diseases, so want to make sure that what they buy is 100 percent safe. A lot of the stock is organic but this is no hippie shop: there is actually a sign in the shop window saying »Hippies use side door«.

»We don't sell scented candles,« explains owner Rudy Penando. »We want to escape the stereotype of the vegan.« One of their stickers says »I love vegan junk food« – not what you'd expect from a vegan shop! Rudy proudly presents the latest addition to the stock: vegan boxing gloves. He started out with a vegan clothing company called The Secret Society of Vegans, selling his printed t-shirts from a market stall in Camden for four years.

Then he was struck by a gap in the market: even though the vegan movement had originated in England, there were no vegan shops in the UK. So Rudy set up Vx in 2010. He imports major parts of his stock from the US and Germany because the market there is much bigger, offering a lot of things unavailable in the UK. Vegans love the shop because of the variety of products they can get there which they wouldn't be able to find in a normal supermarket. There are some crazy things here: give your dog a vegan treat or try the amaretto or tea-flavoured lip balm. You can indeed be cool and vegan at the same time!

Address 73 Caledonian Road, N1 9BT, Tel. +44(0)2078332315, www.vegancross.com | Public Transport Circle, Hammersmith, Metropolitan, Northern, Piccadilly, Victoria Line, Stop King's Cross | Opening Hours Mon 11am–7.30pm, Tues–Sun 10am–6.30pm | Tip Take a walk along Regent's Canal and admire the fountain in front of Central Saint Martin's College of Arts and Design (especially at night)!

107 __ Wears London

Best of London

Historic Greenwich Market, which has up to 120 stalls selling antiques, craft and collectables, is a perfect location for showing the best that young London-based fashion designers have to offer.

Amanda Hancox opened Wears London in November 2013. When she came to London over three years ago, she fell in love with all the small fashion stalls and sellers in Greenwich Market, Camden Lock, Spitalfields, Brick Lane and Covent Garden. Most of these London based designers couldn't afford to open a shop or even create a website – an opportunity Amanda decided she wanted to give them. The first thing she did was establish an online market place, where the designers were listed according to market and customers could buy their clothes online. She also created space on the website for young designers who weren't affiliated to a specific market. Realising it would be even better to have a permanent location in order to give feedback to the designers and connect with customers, she decided to open the shop in Greenwich Market.

Amanda is an accountant by trade and was thus not afraid to manage the financial side of the business. One example of the London fashion talent she promotes is Sophie Postma's label »Reclaim Bags«, bags made using recycled rubber and old tyres, which Sophie developed when still at fashion college. Liberty Keller is a set designer who turned to making simple but elegant tweed jackets.

Menswear designer Laura Lodge stands behind »Reborn London«, a label producing reconstituted, organic men's shirts and t-shirts. The shoe designer Sarah Watkinson-Yull is one of the few manufacturers of high-heeled shoes in Britain and received funding from the Prince's Trust. Another local label from Hackney is »Voilà le vélo«, producing very pretty retro knickers. With all this amazing talent, it is no wonder Amanda is now dreaming of taking the best of London's small fashion designers to other UK cities as well.

Address 9a Greenwich Market, SE10 9HZ, www.wears-london.co.uk,
info@wears-london.co.uk | Public Transport DLR towards Lewisham, Stop Cutty Sark |
Opening Hours Mon–Sun 10.30am–6.30pm | Tip There's a wealth of museums here, but
do you know the Fan Museum (12 Crooms Hill)?

108___ Whitechapel Bell Foundry

The square hole

It's hard to believe that a place that actually makes bells still exists in London, but it does: Whitechapel Bell Foundry in East London, set up in 1570, is Britain's oldest manufacturing company. It moved to its current location, a beautiful Georgian house, in 1738. In 1904 Arthur Hughes purchased the business, and it is still in the possession of the Hughes family.

Arthur's descendent Alan Hughes and his wife Kathryn are joint owners of the foundry today. In the last 500 years it has built many famous bells, among them the clock bells for St. Paul's in 1709, the Liberty Bell in Pennsylvania in 1752, and Big Ben in 1858. While it's wonderful to be able to look back on this amazing history, Kathryn Hughes is also well aware of modern-day necessities, and in November 2013 she launched an online store for bells. Although the foundry's major income still comes from big church bells, they also produce bells in smaller sizes: gift bells, servant bells, door bells, clock bells or musical hand bells, all unique and made on the premises. They use 80 percent copper and 20 percent tin, which makes the bell ring, but also means it breaks easily. Bells are commissioned not only by churches and institutions, but also by individual customers, like the Brazilian gentleman who commissioned a one and a half ton bell for his estate, or a couple who bought a pair of hand bells for their wedding, tuned to the notes of their initials.

The foundry also made eight bells for the Queen's Jubilee pageant named Elizabeth, Philip, Charles, Anne … Although the foundry employs 24 highly specialised craftsmen such as blacksmiths or handbell tuners, it is still a small family business; usually everyone who comes to work here joins the family and stays for the rest of his or her life. As an employee once said: »You can't fit a square peg in a round hole, but we are the square hole!«

Address 32 – 34 Whitechapel Road, E1 1DY, Tel. +44(0)2072472599, www.whitechapelbellfoundry.co.uk, bells@whitechapelbellfoundry.co.uk | **Public Transport** Circle, District, Hammersmith Line, Stop Whitechapel | **Opening Hours** Mon – Fri 9am – 5pm | **Tip** Visit the Whitechapel Gallery (77 – 78 Whitechapel High Street) to look at contemporary art!

109___The Widescreen Centre

The universe from Regent's Park

When you hear Marylebone you may think of Sherlock Holmes, Madame Tussaud's or maybe Harley Street, where a lot of doctors and medical organisations have gathered. But have you heard of the »Baker Street Irregular Astronomers«? This central London astronomical society was founded in 2010. Interested stargazers meet once a month in Regent's Park for an informal star party. Behind this group is the dedicated team of the Widescreen Centre, a specialist shop in Dorset Street where an astronomer will find everything he or she needs to observe the sky.

They are the only astronomical outlet in London and stock a range of telescopes, starting with models for children and beginners and going up to highly professional equipment used by research observatories. Some of the telescopes are computerised and can find specific objects for you in the sky or connect to your smartphone. Other products include binoculars and microscopes, solar telescopes or spotting scopes for bird watching. They also stock a range of 3D products, including monitors, viewers and glasses or 3D lenses that can be used with normal photo cameras. In their motion picture division they offer various film formats and can telecine your old Super-8 films into Quick Time Files or transfer them directly to a hard drive.

The Widescreen Centre opened in 1971. It is a small family business run by Dr. Simon Bennett and his wife Elena Kostyaeva. Simon took over the business in 2003. He met his wife, who had her own company exporting Russian optical devices, at an exhibition. Elena usually comes to the monthly stargazing meeting at »The Hub« in Regent's Park, but doesn't watch the sky much on her own. So why not give it a go – you don't even have to bring your own equipment! Check out the website of the Baker Street Irregular Astronomers at www.bakerstreetastro.org.uk for dates and times and discover the universe from Regent's Park!

Address 47 Dorset Street, W1U 7ND, Tel. +44(0)2079352580,
www.widescreen-centre.co.uk, simon@widescreen-centre.co.uk | Public Transport Baker-
loo, Circle, Hammersmith, Jubilee, Metropolitan Line, Stop Baker Street | Opening Hours
Mon–Fri 9.30am–5.30pm, Thurs 9.30am–7pm, Sat 10am–4pm | Tip Have a coffee and
sandwiches next door in the Nordic Bakery (48 Dorset Street)!

110 — W. Martyn

The aroma of freshly roasted coffee

If you want to find the tea and coffee specialist W. Martyn on Muswell Hill Broadway, just follow the wafting aroma of freshly ground coffee! Once there, you will immediately see where the scent comes from: the old-fashioned 1950s roasting machine in the window.

The shop was founded in 1897 by William Martyn as a general grocer's. The original interiors and mahogany cabinets are still the same as in the 1890s. In those days customers would come in with a list. All their orders would be gathered and delivered directly to their houses the following morning by horse and cart. With the arrival of the supermarkets, the business started to specialise in coffees, teas and fine food. Today it is run in the fourth generation by another William Martyn. William has grown up among nuts and dried fruit. He knows many stories about the shop, like the one of his great aunt playing among the Christmas crackers in the nursery.

Today he tries to sell the products of as many small English businesses as possible, such as the lovely English boiled sweets and toffees. A lady from East Finchley makes chutneys, jams and cakes for them and uses ingredients grown in East Finchley. The hot sauces from Cottage Delight, like the Mexican Hot & Sweet Jalapeño Sauce, are famous among the shop's customers. W. Martyn sells its own signature coffee blends as well as many flavoured coffees, ranging from Cinnamon and Hazel to Irish cream or Christmas coffee. The teas are blended by their tea expert, who does their main blends as well as adding to the selection by trying out new things. Like in the olden days, they sell loose dried fruit and nuts, which look beautiful in the decorated shop window, especially at Christmas time.

William is proud of his heritage and already has the fifth generation waiting in the wings, although his son is only twelve at the moment. It may be some time before he is the one to let the coffee aromas waft across the High Street!

Address 135 Muswell Hill Broadway, N10 3RS, Tel. +44(0)2088835642, www.wmartyn.co.uk, sales@wmartyn.co.uk | **Public Transport** Northern Line, Stop Highgate, then take bus 134 to Muswell Hill | **Opening Hours** Mon–Sat 9.30am–5.30pm, Sun 12pm–4pm | **Tip** Walk down Muswell Hill Road until you come to Queen's Wood, an area of ancient woodland, where you can observe three species of woodpeckers.

111 __ W. Sitch

Making brass lamps since the extinction of the dinosaurs

This specialist shop for metal lamps and chandeliers has existed in Berwick Street since the 1870s. The origins of the family business, which today is managed by Ronald Sitch and his sons James and Laurence, go back even further to the year 1776. Some sources even mention a Sitch who made candlesticks outside the walls of London around 1540!

Five floors filled to the ceiling with metallic lamps and chandeliers – this is the kingdom of Ronald Sitch and his sons. Here you can see wall lamps, ceiling lamps, candelabras, lamps and chandeliers à la Adams and Louis XV. or in the Flemish style. They also still have a forge with cast-iron machines, some of them as old as the chandeliers.

Except for the casting – they stopped doing foundry work after the clean air act of 1956 – they do everything else: put the separate parts together, wire them, weld them together and polish them. W. Sitch reproduces old models, often their own originally made by one of their ancestors, but they also sell antique chandeliers. They never throw anything away, even if it is only a small part of a lamp – it could come in useful one day!

A lot of the Titanic's light fittings were made here, and when the film of the same name was made the set designers came here with photographs and Sitch indeed still had the model. Most of their new lamps are custom-made. They light theatres or old-fashioned gentlemen's clubs; the church St. Mary Magdalene in Paddington ordered 15 chandeliers from them, which they have just finished. For Laurence, commissions like this are the best because they challenge his knowledge and craftsmanship. The next commission might be lights for a library, a concert hall or a millionaire's villa. According to Laurence, W. Sitch »has been making lamps out of brass since the dinosaurs died out« and hopefully will continue to do so for the foreseeable future.

Address 48 Berwick Street, W1F 8JD, Tel. +44 (0)2074373776, www.wsitch.co.uk, info@wsitch.co.uk | Public Transport Bakerloo, Central, Victoria Line, Stop Oxford Circus | Opening Hours Mon–Fri 9am–5pm, Sat 9.30am–1pm | Tip Seize the opportunity and explore the cloth shops that are characteristic of Berwick Street.

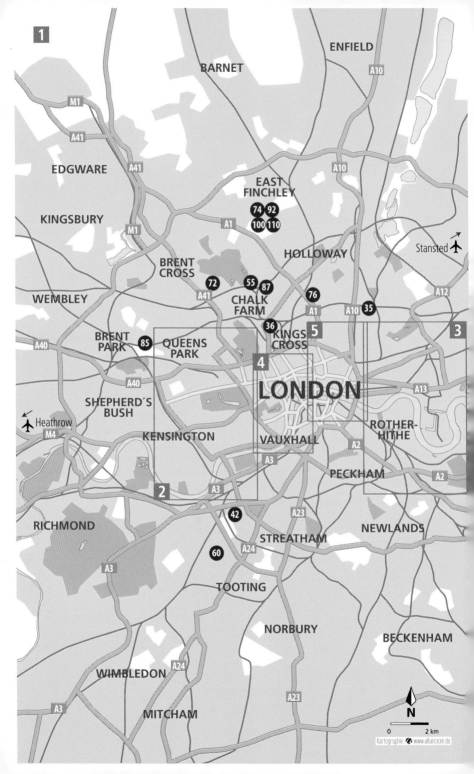

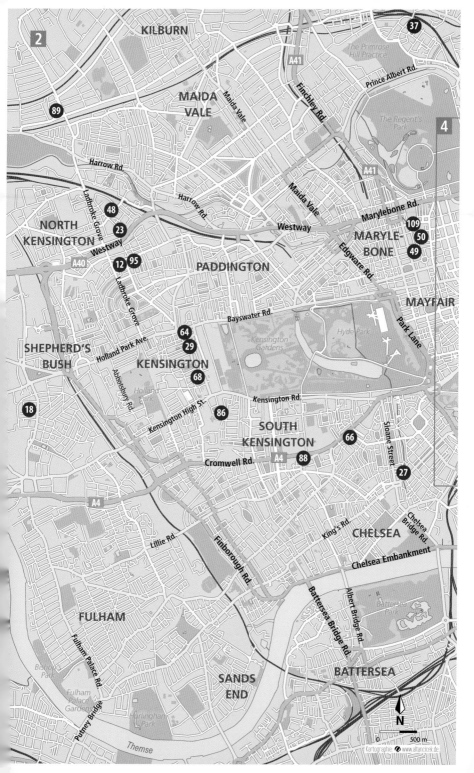

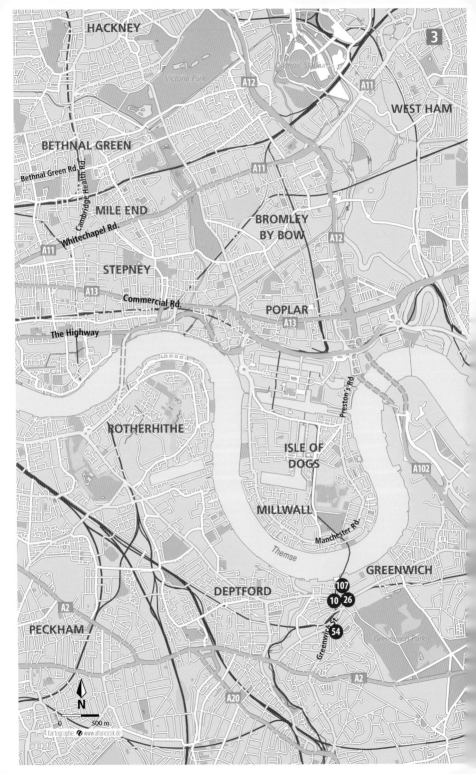

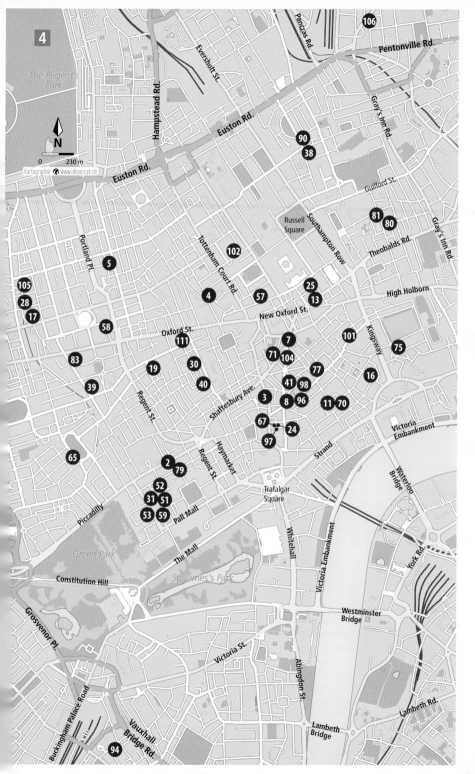

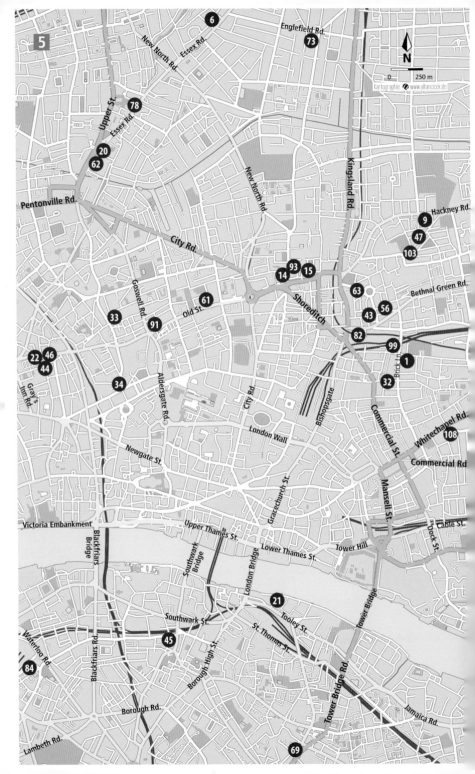

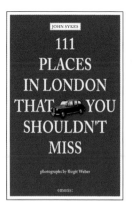

John Sykes
**111 PLACES IN LONDON THAT YOU
SHOULDN'T MISS**
ISBN 978-3-95451-346-8

Lucia Jay von Seldeneck, Carolin Huder,
Verena Eidel
**111 PLACES IN BERLIN THAT YOU
SHOULDN'T MISS**
ISBN 978-3-95451-208-9

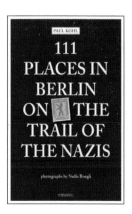

Paul Kohl
**111 PLACES IN BERLIN ON THE
TRAIL OF THE NAZIS**
ISBN 978-3-95451-323-9

Rike Wolf
111 PLACES IN HAMBURG THAT YOU SHOULDN'T MISS
ISBN 978-3-95451-234-8

Rüdiger Liedtke
111 PLACES IN MUNICH THAT YOU SHOULDN'T MISS
ISBN 978-3-95451-222-5

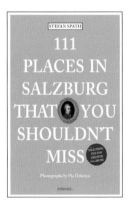

Stefan Spath
111 PLACES IN SALZBURG THAT YOU SHOULDN'T MISS
ISBN 978-3-95451-230-0